Kids, Classrooms, and Capitol Hill

A Peek Inside the Walls of America's Public Schools

KELLY FLYNN

ROWMAN & LITTLEFIELD EDUCATION
Lanham • New York • Toronto • Plymouth, UK

Published in the United States of America
by Rowman & Littlefield Education
A Division of Rowman & Littlefield Publishers, Inc.
A wholly owned subsidiary of The Rowman & Littlefield Publishing Group, Inc.
4501 Forbes Boulevard, Suite 200, Lanham, Maryland 20706
www.rowmaneducation.com

Estover Road
Plymouth PL6 7PY
United Kingdom

Author represented by Educational Design Services Literary Agency.

British Library Cataloguing in Publication Information Available

Library of Congress Cataloging-in-Publication Data

Flynn, Kelly, 1958–
  Kids, classrooms, and Capitol Hill / Kelly Flynn.
    p. cm.
  ISBN-13: 978-1-57886-822-3 (cloth : alk. paper)
  ISBN-10: 1-57886-822-X (cloth : alk. paper)
  1. Education, Secondary—United States. 2. Public schools—United States. 3.
Education and state—United States. 4. Educational change—United States. I. Title.
  LA196.F59 2008
  373.73—dc22

                                                                2008007138

⊗™ The paper used in this publication meets the minimum requirements of
American National Standard for Information Sciences—Permanence of Paper for
Printed Library Materials, ANSI/NISO Z39.48-1992.
Manufactured in the United States of America.

For the Teachers

Contents

Preface

For the most part, the hearts of all teachers beat with compassion, kindness, and a strong sense of fair play. They are often similar in their politics, their lifestyles, and their views of the world.

But after six years of talking with teachers from all over the country, I've learned that they hold philosophical differences on many educational issues. For example, a few years ago a school district in the Flint, Michigan, area asked a teacher to learn to give EpiPen injections to a student. Another teacher was asked to learn to administer insulin shots. To me, the idea was horrifying; far too much responsibility, with too much room for error. Don't get me wrong—if a student needs an EpiPen injection or an insulin shot, then the district needs to be prepared to give it—which is why it should be a federally funded mandate that every single school building have a full-time nurse on staff.

But while many teachers agreed with me, maintaining that if they had wanted to give shots they would have gone to nursing school, many others told me they were happy to do it. They said they were willing to learn anything, or do anything, that would help their students in the classroom.

These philosophical differences are fascinating to me. Teachers are all working toward the exact same goal—educating kids—and yet they sometimes have surprisingly different ideas about how to get there.

Should teachers use treats as rewards? Some say yes, some say no. What about tracking, the practice of channeling students into classes based on ability? That was a giant point of contention between teachers in my

English department. Even the appropriate amount of homework is up for debate between teachers.

Teachers tell me that, like Monday morning quarterbacks, they discuss my Sunday newspaper column—sometimes heatedly—in their lounges the next day. And so, to foster these conversations between teachers, and those involved in teacher preparation—professors and their students—discussion prompts are included at the end of the book.

Ultimately, teachers agree more than they disagree. And they are definitely in agreement on the significant issues: that it is difficult to teach a child who is hungry, that kids learn better when they receive individual attention, and that education and a love of learning begin at home, long before kindergarten.

There is a huge disconnect between what is really going on in schools, and what the public thinks is going on in schools. And that disconnect renders most education reform, useless. So, to that end, these prompts are useful for everyone with a stake in education—parents, taxpayers, lawmakers, and policy makers.

There are no right or wrong answers to these prompts. They are meant merely to encourage readers to think about the issues, and to learn from the viewpoints of others.

Educators—the ones standing in front of the students every day—need to assert themselves in discussions on education reform. The public needs to listen.

Let the dialogue begin.

Kelly Flynn
February 2008

Special Thanks

I must begin by thanking Paul Keep, the former editor of *The Flint Journal* (current editor and publisher of *The Muskegon Chronicle*), because it is his open-mindedness that allowed my newspaper column to be. Six years ago I pitched him the idea of a weekly column about education from a teacher's point of view, and he listened. Sure, there are education writers, and education columnists, but few, if any, have actually taught in a public school. Paul recognized the fresh perspective a former teacher could bring to education coverage. He is a man with vision and, truly, just a prince of a guy.

Thank you to my agent, Bertram Linder, for recognizing the broad appeal of this material and finding it a home. Thank you to Tom Koerner, my editor at Rowman & Littlefield, his assistant Paul Cacciato, and Lynda Phung, my production editor, for their patience, and guidance, as I learned about the publishing process.

"Just read it one more time, pleeeeeease," are words my husband, Norman Falconer, has heard every single week for the last six years. And every single week for the last six years he has graciously dropped whatever he was doing to read it, one more time. When Norman retired after thirty years in the classroom he was ready to leave the world of education behind. But he lets me drag him back, into every sort of philosophical discussion about teaching, learning, and the politics of education. Though he's happiest swinging a hammer, he's an excellent editor, too. I am infinitely grateful for his multitalented brilliance, and for all the times he has saved me from putting my foot squarely in my mouth.

I'd like to thank my sister Kerry Flynn, cheerleader extraordinaire. Actually, she's an athlete, not a cheerleader, but she is a cheerleader for me. I couldn't have a more perfect sister if I had picked her out of a catalog. How lucky I am to move through this life knowing that someone so strong, smart, funny, and good-natured has always got my back.

Thank you to my delightful sister-in-law, Denise Kabisch, for taking the author photo for this book.

Thank you to my mom, Betty Flynn, who told me from the beginning that I must have the courage to say the unpopular thing if it was a truth that needed to be said. And thank you to my dad, Dennis Flynn, who taught me by example absolutely everything there is to know about optimism. And thanks to both of them for teaching me from an early age not to give a fig what anyone thinks or says about me. That lesson has served me well as classroom teacher where a thick skin is essential, and ironically, as a newspaper columnist, too. It is truly a gift of freedom.

And of course, my most sincere thanks to the teachers. To my own teachers, to the teachers I taught with, and to the teachers I affectionately call my "peeps," the ones who meet me in my virtual teachers' lounge and generously share their successes and their frustrations about the murky world of teaching.

This book is for every teacher in every kind of classroom, large, small, rural, urban, suburban, public, private, charter. You are heroes every day.

Most important, my deepest gratitude to the Universe, from whence all inspiration comes.

Introduction

It was second hour and we were in lockdown mode. "Lockdown" was a term we became uneasily familiar with in the post-Columbine era. It meant that teachers and students were locked into their classrooms because some sort of threat had been made toward the school or someone in it.

We, of course, had no idea what that threat was. We just knew that no one could enter or leave the classrooms, even to go to the bathroom, until the all-clear signal was given. The fact that we couldn't leave meant that immediately every student wanted to, desperately. We all felt anxious, restless, and trapped.

As I sat with my second hour students, and second hour dragged into third, I thought about how the public just really doesn't "get" the public school experience today. Sure, there would be a short, dry news story about the incident in the paper, but it wouldn't come close to describing how we felt, trapped in that room wondering what the heck was going on, half listening for gunshots or explosions.

It was then that the idea for my newspaper column was born. I knew that newspaper coverage of education always seemed to slightly miss the mark. I also knew that I seldom saw teachers quoted in news stories. And I knew why, from listening to the teachers in my lounge. They would rather face a month of cafeteria duty than be quoted in a news story. Teachers are rabidly protective of their schools, and their school's reputations. They worry about saying the wrong thing and tarnishing the profession, or being perceived as unprofessional.

They're also just flat out too busy to pay much attention to anything that happens outside of their classrooms. Add to that the fact that most education reporters don't understand the issues well enough to ask the right questions to tell the real story, and you have very shallow education coverage.

I had been keeping a teaching journal that year, mostly as a way to vent my frustration at the absurdity of the mandates that were handed down to classroom teachers. Drawing from that journal I created a set of newspaper columns and pitched the idea of an education column from a teacher's point of view to the editor of our city paper, *The Flint Journal*.

The first weekly column ran on September 12, 2002, in *The Grand Blanc News*, a small community paper owned by Booth Newspapers, *The Flint Journal*'s parent company. A few weeks later it ran in all eight of the community newspapers, owned by Booth and published by *The Flint Journal*. Six months later it was moved to the Sunday op-ed page of *The Journal*, where it has been for six years. The column was also picked up by another city paper, the *Jackson Citizen Patriot* in Jackson, Michigan, where it ran for three years.

This book is a collection of the most timeless of these columns, the ones teachers most often request copies of.

But this book is not just for teachers. Parents find this material fascinating, too, because they get to see a teacher's point of view. They don't always like it, but they are curious and interested in it. I say things that are not likely to be said to a parent by a teacher. But they are things that it would be useful for parents to know.

We cannot "reform" education until we see it clearly. And too much of the current reform assumes that kids come to school ready and willing to learn, that they sit at their desks straight and tall, polite and orderly. Current education reform rarely acknowledges the depth and variety of personal challenges faced by students, and the people who teach them. To that end, this book should be read by anyone with a stake in the future of education in this country: taxpayers, legislators, and policy makers.

Teachers tell me—usually in amazement—that the column is right on target. What they're used to reading about themselves in mainstream media is largely inaccurate.

This is a side of the story that is never told. Almost all education coverage in the mainstream media is told from an outsider looking in.

I tell the story from the inside looking out.

CHAPTER 1

Teachers

AN INTERESTING BREED

So, What's Going On behind Those High School Walls

"I don't have a pencil!"

"I lost my book!"

"This class is boring!"

"This school *sucks*!"

After almost twenty years in a high school classroom (and hearing these comments twenty times a day), I started to question my sanity. I knew it was time to get out.

Too young to retire, too old to get a job as the TV weather girl, I knew I had to make a career change before they either carried me out in a straightjacket or I got twenty to life. So I jumped ship.

I was badly in need of some career counseling, but the secretary in our career center said I didn't qualify for a day-on-the-job.

So I turned to my first true love—journalism. I've been in love with the world of journalism since my days at Michigan State University. And as a journalism teacher and student newspaper adviser, I have had the privilege of coaching some brilliant young writers.

Some say that those who can, do, and those who can't, teach. I don't think that's true, so I took a shot and now I'm walking the walk after twenty years of talking the talk.

My intention with this book is to give you a peek inside the walls of a public school. Chances are you won't hear this point of view from the people you know who are actually working in schools, because if there is one thing educators are afraid of, it's that they'll say the wrong thing and appear unprofessional. So they spout the party line and make nice, zealously guarding the truth and the reputations of their school.

And the truth is this: this thing called education is complicated, messy, excruciatingly difficult, humbling, aggravating beyond belief, and fleetingly rewarding.

Many of you haven't spent time in a classroom since you were students. I plan to take you inside and show you around. I'll explore the issues, big and small, facing the key players in what sometimes feels like an impossible quest—educating teenagers.

The players haven't changed much.

Teenagers: They are simultaneously the most charming and the most annoying people on the planet. One minute they are hiding behind a flat-eyed, curled-lip insolence that could stop a Navy Seal dead in his tracks. In the next minute they will bring you to tears with their vulnerability and kindness.

Administrators: Alzheimer's runs rampant. The minute they become administrators most of them forget what it was like when they were classroom teachers themselves. Worse yet, some were hired as administrators without classroom experience.

Teachers: Brave, tenacious, and world-weary, they struggle to teach the required curriculum while wearing several hats at once—disciplinarian, parent, social worker, counselor, psychologist, referee. No one in America has been lied to more, except perhaps a cop or a Senate investigating committee.

Parents: These are the real power players in the equation.

When it comes to public education, what parents want, parents get. They are the customers, and the customer is always right. This can be a good thing, for example, when they rally support for a failing band program. But it's a bad, bad thing when one parent can undermine a school discipline policy.

Politicians: They shamelessly use education as a bargaining chip in their game of politics. They hold the purse strings and give lip service to education, but rarely make a positive difference in day-to-day teaching and learning.

School Board: This is a mixed breed, a cross between politicians and administrators. At best they care deeply about their district. At worst, they are operating purely from ego to satisfy a personal power trip or political aspiration.

So this is it. The nitty-gritty, down and dirty side of public education. It's not for the faint of heart.

We Always Recognize One of Our Own

It's 5 a.m. I'm sitting in my office in the dark, quietly working at the computer, trying not to wake anyone. I'm pondering this new life I have now that I am no longer a teacher, when I happen to catch a glimpse of myself reflected in the shiny brass apple that I was given by my school district when I left.

And suddenly, when I see my reflection in that shiny apple, I realize that I still see myself as a teacher. I started playing school with the neighbor kids when I was five years old, and I will always and forever be a teacher at heart.

Because, you see, you can take the teacher out of the classroom, but you can't take the classroom out of the teacher.

We teachers are an interesting breed. A Gallup poll says that teachers are the most highly trusted group of professionals. I'm glad to hear that, but I'm surprised, too, considering the beating the public school system, and teachers, take in the media.

People make assumptions about you when they find out that you're a teacher. They start acting funny, self-consciously, the way they might around a nun, or a minister.

For one thing, they immediately assume that you're a goody-two-shoes. They apologize for swearing around you, as if they're afraid you might send them to the principal's office. They wait until you've left the room to tell the latest dirty joke.

And they always pull you aside to tell you their own school woes. They explain their personal learning difficulties, describe the teachers they loved, and the teachers they hated.

I'm not sure what it is about teachers, but we can always recognize one of our own. One time my husband, a retired career teacher, and I were having dinner at a local pub. At the table next to us a group of adults were enjoying happy hour. We glanced over, then looked back at each other knowingly. "Wonder what school district they're from?" my husband asked.

We puzzled over our mutual assumption for a minute. How did we instantly know they were teachers? What tipped us off? We finally decided that teachers have a certain aura of control about them. You just know that if a fire broke out, they would be the first out of their seats, directing people out of the burning building.

Teachers are keen observers, always aware of their surroundings. And they're always conscious of being observed, too.

Teachers have no qualms about telling kids to behave, either—even if they're not our own. One time while grocery shopping with my husband, we heard a little boy loudly arguing with his mother three aisles away. Mom had no control and the kid was being a brat. He escaped and came skipping down the aisle we were standing in, sliding to a stop in front of us.

"HEY! You mind your mother!" barked my husband. The kid's eyes popped in surprise and fear, and he turned on his heel and ran. All was quiet after that.

Hustling through the mall one time I came to a group of women standing and chatting, right smack dab in the middle of the aisle. It took every ounce of self-restraint I had not to bellow, "Move along ladies! Don't block the road, please!"

Another time, my husband and I were in a movie theater, and five minutes into the movie, four kids came in, about thirteen to fourteen years old. They proceeded to laugh and talk out loud, standing up, changing seats, and kicking the seats of the people in front of them. People were getting really annoyed and shooting dirty looks their way. Suddenly, a man a few seats away turned to them and said, loudly and sternly, "Excuse me. Are we interrupting you here? Sit down and don't make another sound!" The startled kids sat down and *didn't* make another sound.

On the way out of the theater we found ourselves walking next to this same man. I raised my eyebrows inquiringly.

"Teacher?" I asked.

"Yeah," he sighed.

I nodded in understanding.

And Yes, We Do Have Super Powers

Sometimes I heard the most amazing things in my classroom.

"Hey, Steve, I heard you had another party this weekend."

"Yeah, man, I did. My parents were out of town again. It was great!"

"Dude, how do you get away with it? You have more parties than anyone I know. Don't your neighbors tell your parents?"

"Oh, no, man, 'cause I use the signs."

"The signs? What signs?"

"You know, the birthday signs. I made these big signs, you know, like you make for someone's birthday, poster board stapled to a stick. I use markers and make the letters all fancy, then I stick the sign in the ground in my yard on the day of the party. In between, I keep the signs under my mattress so my Mom doesn't find them."

"Well, what do the signs say?"

"This week it said, 'Happy 50th Birthday Aunt Bertha!' See, the neighbors think it's a family party for some old lady. It's genius, man!"

This conversation took place in the workroom attached to the back of my classroom. I was sitting at my desk in the front of the room, thirty feet away. I didn't want to hear it, but there's no escaping the Super Powers.

Oh, didn't you know? Teachers have Super Powers. Years of hearing and seeing it all have honed our senses and instincts to super hero levels.

Supersonic hearing is just one of our Super Powers. We can also spot the same answer on two student's papers, even if they're from a different hour and we grade them several hours apart. We can tell by the handwriting whether a paper belongs to a boy or a girl, and usually know exactly which of our 130 students it belongs to. Super elastic bladders allow us to go six hours without a bathroom break. And we can spot a lie almost before it's uttered.

During a test we know which kid is asking his neighbor for a pencil, and which one is asking for an answer. We know when a kid really has to use the bathroom, and when he just wants to go for a walk. We know when a kid doesn't understand something, even if she says she does. We can even sense when a fight is going to break out in a high school.

One time, on my way to the office to do a couple of errands before school started, I saw Ricky Warchawski standing in front of an open locker with about six girls clustered around him. Ricky was this bigger-than-life character, not only in size, but in spirit and enthusiasm and energy. Loud.

Playful. Kind. He was one of those rare kids who is part of no clique, but welcome in all, easily crossing social lines because of his open, good heart.

I was in a hurry and moving fast.

As I approached I could see that Ricky was holding something carefully in his hand. At about five feet away I realized that it was a clear plastic baggie and that there was something in it.

Something moving.

I was really hustling, so I didn't slow down.

"Whatcha got in the bag, Ricky?" I asked.

"Crickets!" he boomed. "Want one?!" and he took a cricket out of the bag and held it out to me. (Why did he have a baggie full of crickets? I don't know. Sometimes, you just don't ask.)

"No, thanks, not today," I said, smiling. By now I was right even with him, and he took the cricket and waved it in the girls' faces. Of course they squealed.

I sailed on by. Without looking back or even breaking stride I said over my shoulder, "And take it out of your mouth, please."

Full-blown screams. "Eewwww! How did you know he was going to *do* that?!" the girls squealed. I glanced back just in time to see Ricky pull the cricket out of his mouth.

Yep, it's true. We have eyes in the backs of our heads, too.

The First Year Is the Toughest

There can't be a job on earth as hard as the first year of teaching. It's an initiation by fire, a marathon sprint to June, with no letup and not a moment for contemplation or reflection.

Self-doubt. Frustration. Exhaustion.

I remember it well.

My first year of teaching was the year from hell. So bad, in fact, that I can't believe I ever went back.

Initially, I was assigned five sections of freshman English. Not bad, I thought. I can focus on one thing and get really good at it.

Meanwhile, a more senior teacher complained about my one-prep schedule. Twenty-four hours later he had mine and I had his: Eighth Grade Reading Lab, Ninth Grade Reading Lab, Writing Lab, and Yearbook. I was a brand-new teacher with four preps that included a student publication.

The reading and writing labs were full of poor readers and low achievers, including nineteen special education students, even more than the special ed. teachers were allowed to have on their cascloads.

I walked into my classroom the first day, unprepared for the cold stares of tough looking kids. I was terrified.

But wait. It gets worse.

A new reading program was being piloted down the street at the Genesee Intermediate School District (GISD), and our superintendent decreed that we would participate. Three hours of instruction later, I was put in charge.

My days became one long race against the clock. I arrived at school at 6:30 a.m. to get in some quiet work time. Then I boarded a school bus with my students, and raced to the GISD to spend forty minutes on the computers. We rushed back onto the bus, back to the school, and I taught an hour in my classroom.

Yearbook class included a $10,000 contract with a company that required me to create, publish, sell, and distribute eight hundred copies of a book.

Then back to the bus with another class, back to the GISD, race through the lesson, back to the bus, and back to school in time to meet my last class in my classroom.

To top it all off, we had record rainfall that year, and I spent part of each day standing in it, taking roll as my kids got on and off the bus. I was terrified that I would lose a student along the way.

It was grueling. Sheer stubbornness kept me going.

I also experienced my first really mean, possibly unstable, parent. In phone call after phone call she issued orders and ultimatums. She told me to move her daughter's seat. I complied. Angrily, she demanded to know why I moved her daughter's seat. On and on it went, her emotional rollercoaster holding me hostage. All semester I fielded calls from her, doing my best to be professional, but secretly worrying that she might somehow get me fired.

I felt old overnight. My friends were having fun in their first real jobs, and went out to play at the end of the day. I took my work home with me, literally and figuratively. I felt weighted down with responsibility, accountability. Evenings and weekends were spent preparing lessons and grading papers, frantically trying to stay one step ahead of the kids. The low salary didn't bother me. I didn't have time to spend it, anyway.

Not a single thing I learned in college prepared me for that first year. And I learned more that first year on the job than I did in four years of college. The thing that I needed most desperately, classroom management and discipline, had never even been mentioned in my education classes.

Like some sort of screwy boot camp, that year tested my stamina, my professionalism, my psychological stability, and my dedication.

So why did I go back the next year?

I went back because I was sure I could do better. Every year, every class, every lesson, every student, I just kept thinking that I could do better.

You face a lot of failure when you teach. Your students.' And your own.

Every first year teacher faces it.

But right around every corner, there's another opportunity to succeed.

College Didn't Teach Me This

Don't tell my dad, but my expensive college education did not prepare me for the realities of teaching.

I'll never forget my first solo lesson with a Senior English class during my student teaching stint.

I was so ready. New shoes, perfectly typed handouts cold off the mimeograph machine, a change-the-world attitude, and a lovingly prepared lesson plan.

I enthusiastically launched into that lesson.

Whisperwhisperwhisperwhisper.

What in the world? I looked around in surprise.

Whisperwhisperwhisperwhisper.

I stopped and waited, pinpointing the whisperers with a hard look. They quieted.

I smiled and continued.

Whisperwhisperwhisperwhisper.

What the heck?! They weren't even listening. Why weren't they listening? Why weren't they hanging on every word of this fabulous lesson?! And why hadn't someone warned me about this?! *Now* what?!

Well, eventually, through trial and error, I did learn techniques for getting their attention and making them listen (or at least be quiet while I talked). But unfortunately, that was just the first of many of the Things No

One Told Me About Teaching. I experienced a few other rude awakenings, too:

- No one told me I would be transformed overnight from a fun-loving college coed to a world-weary fuddy-duddy who (gladly) went to bed at 8:30 p.m. every night. It happens to all of us. I remember sitting in the teachers' lounge with another new teacher, a former college cheerleader, life-of-the-party kind of gal and chuckling at her plaintive cry: "What's happened to me? I used to be *fun!*"
- No one told me that when it comes to the copy machine, it's every woman for herself, and that even if you arrive at 6:30 a.m. you'll still have to stand in line. They also didn't tell me that I would spend half of my time at said copy machine on my hands and knees with my fanny in the air, trying not to get black gunk on my clothes while I tried in vain to un-jam it.
- No one told me how dirty schools are, and that I would eventually give up my professional-looking suits for a wash-and-wear wardrobe. That I would trade in my heels for flats, so that I could sprint down the hall in pursuit of the kids who ignored my request to remove their hats, or throw away their soft drinks.
- No one told me that I was entering a profession where the biggest perk would be a plastic chip-clip or a refrigerator magnet, given to me by my teaching association on National Teacher's Day.
- No one told me that I would need to grow a reptilian-thick skin, to protect myself from the sheer meanness of teenagers, their parents, and the public.
- No one told me that feelings of helplessness and heartbreak would sometimes overwhelm me when I saw the poor, neglectful, abusive home lives that some of my students came from.
- No one told me that some of these kids aren't kids at all, but rather hardened criminals who don't belong in a school with real kids.
- Everyone talks about summers off. But no one told me that I was entering a profession that would suck the very lifeblood out of me if I let it. No one told me that no matter how much I did, it would never be enough. That when I was done for the day, in addition to the stacks of papers I had to correct, there would be meetings upon meetings upon meetings to attend, kids to tutor, teams to coach, dances to chaperone, clubs to sponsor and theater performances to attend. That administration

would demand more, parents would demand more, students would demand more. No one told me that when you sign on with a school district you might as well keep food in your desk and a change of clothes in your cabinet, because you're never going home again.

The Weight of the World

Someone asked me once what it's like now that I am no longer teaching.

"I feel like the weight of the world has been lifted off my shoulders," I said.

And it's true.

Since I left the classroom I have about 130 fewer things to worry about—130 kids, that is.

People don't become teachers so that they can have summers off. And if they do, they don't stay. The job is just too tough. People choose teaching because they care about kids. But being an authority figure to kids hell-bent on bucking authority makes it difficult for kids to see that.

I was shocked when a former student told me that she had no idea that her teachers ever gave a thought to their students outside of the school day. She thought teachers didn't feel *any* emotion toward their students except, perhaps, occasionally anger.

That couldn't be further from the truth.

Because when it comes to kids, teachers are like a woman in a bad country song, standing by her man. No matter how obnoxious the student, we believe *we'll* be the one to make a difference, to save him, to turn him around, and we spend a lot of time planning how.

We obsess about our students. We lose sleep over them. We think about them at home, on the weekends, vacations, and during the summer.

In fact, most teachers, despite our demeanor, feel parental toward our students, worrying about the same things a parent does: their safety, whether they're drinking or using drugs, falling in with the wrong crowd, their feelings and self-esteem.

Above all, though, we worry about their education. Teachers care deeply about whether or not their students learn.

Do we get grouchy? Yes. Do we get overwhelmed? Absolutely. Do we ever feel like throwing in the towel and taking a job at Kmart? Oh, yeah.

But most of us don't. Most of us buck up and do it again the next day, the next year, trying a little harder, scheming and plotting how to *do it better*. We're not all good at showing how much we care. For some of us, the warm fuzzies don't come easily. But when push comes to shove, even the gruffest among us would go to bat for a student in need, even one who has made it his business to be as unlikable as possible. I have seen teachers go above and beyond in all kinds of situations, providing tutoring, time, money, transportation, food, clothing, and even shelter.

The mother of one of my students said it best. Her ninth grade son was acting up in my class and when I put my foot down, he complained to his mother that I was picking on him.

And this wise woman said to him, "Son, there's not a single adult in that school who does not have your best interests at heart. I do not believe that this teacher is picking on you."

Well said, Mom.

The Lounge Is a Stinky Haven

There's something mysterious in the public school system that students never see and the public knows little about.

It's the teachers' lounge.

Most people think it's a place for grading papers and writing lesson plans, but to teachers, it's much, much more.

Part haven, part asylum, reeking of stinky feet and old soup, it's a place where teachers can kick off their shoes and sit for a moment. It's a place to grab a bad cup of coffee from a dirty pot, or a cold can of pop from a temperamental machine, though chances are you won't have time to finish either.

Student teachers are cautioned by professors to stay out of the lounge, fearing that negativity is contagious. And in a job where you spend most of your time trying to make kids do something they don't want to do, there is plenty of that. But it's also a place where a rookie can learn from experienced teachers what they weren't taught in college: the subtleties of classroom management and student discipline.

To call it a lounge is a bit of a stretch. Little free time leaves little time for lounging, and most aren't conducive to lounging anyway. As student populations grow in buildings too small, every available space is needed for instruction. So the lounge is usually an afterthought, sporting beat-up, cast-off furniture and tables sticky with yesterday's lunch. Noisy old refrigerators full of furry, forgotten food sit next to ancient microwaves, interiors thick with splattered food and smells—"*my God, who nuked the leftover fish?!*"

From somebody's garden surplus to batches of burned cookies, food left in the lounge is snatched and snarfed quickly—nothing is too old or too gross.

Mice are frequent visitors, though principals are not, conversation tending to stop when they enter. But gripes aired in the lounge make their way to administrators anyway. Not because the lounge is bugged (except for ants and roaches), but because every school has a mole, sucking up to the brass.

A timid knock signals a student at the door and teachers wait each other out to see who will answer it. But shouts and hollers from outside have teachers dropping sandwiches and springing from seats to break up a fight in the hall.

It's a marketplace for trading classroom materials, selling homemade crafts, and hawking your own kid's Girl Scout cookies. And come November, instead of a football pool, teachers buy squares betting on the date of the first snow day.

One person in the wrong chair throws everyone for a loop, disrupting the imaginary seating chart established the first few days of school.

Academic arguments last forever—does a comma go before "and" in a series? Teachers of business and English disagree.

In the sanctuary of the teachers' lounge, I've seen tempers flare and success celebrated. I've seen teachers cry, and I've seen them laugh until they cry.

But one thing's for sure: a few minutes reprieve from students makes all the difference in the world.

One Teacher's Crime Taints Us All

Believe me, there's no glee in this secret. There's no thrill in the hearing, or in the telling of it. In fact, this secret brings such a flood of conflicting emotions that you're at once met with a need to talk about it, and an unwillingness to voice it aloud.

I'm talking about the sickening feeling that teachers feel upon learning that one of their colleagues has been accused of sexual impropriety.

First, disbelief: How could someone we ate lunch with and shared lesson plans with and stood in line for the copy machine with, possibly be guilty of something like . . . *that*? Wouldn't we have suspected? Wouldn't there have been clues? We feel duped and stupid . . . we should have *known*.

Second, empathy: We don't want to believe it because it could be us. We know exactly how vulnerable we are. We know exactly how dangerous an angry student or parent can be. Miffed over a low grade or some perceived slight, students and parents have been known to vindictively make accusations based on almost nothing. Sure, there's an investigation and if you're innocent you'll be proven so. But can a teacher's reputation ever recover? Won't there always be a bit of, "Oh, you know Mr. Smith, the one who was accused of _____"?

Third, revulsion: Sexual impropriety of any kind goes against every instinct we have as teachers—instincts to protect, nurture, and guide. If it's true, and we desperately hope it's not, we want the perpetrator punished to the fullest extent of the law as badly as anyone.

Deep down, we worry that one teacher's crime taints us all. We hate when our profession takes a hit, putting another bullet in the gun of the public school bashers. Some believe that the problem lies with the teachers' unions, that they somehow conspire to protect the unsavory. That's not true, because no matter what your profession, union member or not, you have a right to go through the legal process if accused of a crime.

But most important, though, how could this person have ended up in our midst? Why wasn't there some way to prevent this?

If they've been convicted we *can* prevent them from getting into schools because state lawmakers all over the country have set up "predator free zones" preventing convicted sex offenders from living less than two city blocks from schools. Criminal background checks, including fingerprinting, are required on all new school employees. And the Federal Bureau of Investigation is compiling the National Sex Offenders Registry, coordinating law enforcement agencies and departments of education from every state.

No, our concern isn't how to keep out the convicted sex offenders.

It's how to recognize the ones who are already inside.

Ahh, In-service: I Needed That Nap

Martin Luther King Day still makes me shudder.

You see, in communities, Martin Luther King Day is an opportunity to honor a great American. For students, it's a day off school. But for teachers, it means only one thing: the dreaded *in-service*.

The first problem with in-services is that reluctant teachers who are already juggling too many tasks usually plan them. Administrators strong-arm a few teachers into "volunteering," so after teaching all day they meet and, armed with good intentions, little time, and almost no budget, struggle to plan an enlightening and inspiring day for their colleagues. It's a thankless job.

The second problem with in-services (regardless of who plans them) is that once the educational community comes up with a new "educational theory," they beat it to death. The simplest concept is dragged out interminably. For example, I learned about the Know and Do model of lesson design at an in-service. It's useful, but it's not rocket science. I understood it the first time it was presented to me. I didn't need to be drilled on it repeatedly for the next three years. Do administers think we're slow, or are they that hard-pressed to come up with something new?

The third problem with in-services is that teachers are treated like children instead of professionals. We're often put into groups when we arrive to ensure that we don't sit with our friends. Building principals strategically place themselves around the room so we can't grade papers while we listen. And if we happen to get through the in-service material early, they scramble to fill the time with inane announcements, rather than let us go early.

The most demoralizing thing about in-services, though, is that so much of the time is spent pointing out where we're supposedly not succeeding. Sometimes our students' collective grade point averages are paraded in front of us (they're too low). Sometimes it's standardized test scores (too low, too). Sometimes it's discipline referrals (much too high). "Bam!" goes another nail, right into my teaching spirit's coffin.

The one thing that teachers need more than anything is quiet time to work in their classrooms (on the clock for a change, not after school). They also want time with their colleagues to share lessons and discipline strategies. Truly, sometimes the most you see of the teachers in your department is a wave as you pass in the hall. Yet that seems to be the one thing that administrators and school boards are most loath to give. Instead we're treated as if we can't be trusted with any unstructured time and they pack each in-service full of busywork. There's a strong puritan work ethic in education that fears a few idle minutes.

I'm not saying that there isn't anything new to be learned, and I don't object to learning it. But just like my students, I *do* object to busywork.

So why do we put up with it? Why don't we just put our collective aching feet down? Mostly, it's because teachers are just really polite, follow-the-rules kinds of people.

There's a much more compelling reason, though, an epiphany that came to me after a particularly bad week. I'd inadvertently given too many writing assignments at once and had stacks of essays to grade. I'd had several nerve-racking meetings with parents, and attended three after-school meetings in a row. I was worn out.

And then it hit me. The next day was . . . In-Service Day! Someone else would have to create the lesson, type the handouts, stand on their feet all day, and deliver the material! I could sit and . . . *rest!*

That's why teachers suffer in-services in silence. They're just so blasted grateful to have someone else run the show for a while.

One thing is certain. After an in-service, you're pretty thrilled to get back to your classroom. It can make that really rowdy third hour class look pretty darn good.

Burnout: An Affliction of Secrecy and Denial

They're not going to admit it to you. They probably haven't even admitted it to themselves. But I can assure you that there are teachers you know, right this minute, living lives of quiet desperation.

It's called teacher burnout and it's an affliction of secrecy and denial. In a profession that by its very nature requires you to be upbeat and positive all the time—and in fact offers you no place to hide when you aren't—to not be so is to fail.

And let's face it, society isn't always kind when people admit their weaknesses. A couple of years ago on *Oprah*, new mothers discussed their inability to get into the groove of motherhood. They hadn't felt the bliss that other mothers did. The blissful mothers' unforgiving attitude was, what kind of freak is unhappy with a brand-new baby?

No, society can be unkind to those who don't feel the way they "should."

Which is why, even when overwhelmed by it, teachers often deny their despair. They don't want to look weak or reflect badly on their school. It's depressing and frightening when your calling, no longer is.

Some call teaching the lonely profession because teachers spend their days closed away in classrooms with kids, with little or no contact with adults.

And it's true. When I left teaching people kept asking me, "Won't you miss the people you teach with?" And I had to answer in all honesty, no. Not because they weren't nice people—they were. But you don't miss what you never had. I had no time in my day for chitchat. A quick hello as you race in and out of the bathroom doesn't a friendship make. Even the lunch half-hour leaves little time for collegiality. Many of us ate in our classrooms. I did, so that my journalism students could have more time on the computers.

If you ask most teachers what kind of professional development they want, they'll tell you that they want time to spend with their colleagues, to share teaching and discipline strategies, or to get answers to simple questions like, "What do you do to make prepositions interesting?" or "What do you do when the same kid doesn't have a pencil for the tenth time in a row?"

Feeling like you have no say in decisions that affect you, struggling to make kids care about education, little evidence of accomplishment, and plain and simple exhaustion all lead to burnout.

But once you've spent a great deal of time and money earning several degrees, and have moved up the pay scale, changing careers is daunting.

Too many burned-out teachers stay on the job, detached and not connecting with kids. We need some sort of assistance program for career teachers who don't want to leave, but need help getting their fire relit.

Because if there's no help and they can't leave, unfortunately, they're taking up space where an inspired teacher could be.

Is It Time to Go?

Search your soul teacher: is it time for you to retire?

I know, I know, it's no one's business but your own. And it's a painful, touchy subject.

And I know what you're thinking. When you look around at the new crop of teachers, you're thinking that even on your worst day you're better than most of them. And that may be a little bit true. At least you've got your classroom under control, which is more than can be said for many rookies, right?

But think back. You didn't always have your classroom under control that first year either. That came with experience. You learned that kids are like animals that sense fear—when you quit showing that fear, they quit testing you.

Bet you know your subject better than those newbies, too, don't you? You've had years to steep yourself in your material, and they're barely a chapter ahead of the kids. In time, those things will come to the rookies. But you know as well as I that there's mountains more to good teaching than classroom control and mastery of subject.

Are you still creative, or are you in a rut? Are you using ancient lesson plans and tests? Have you chalked up all new teaching methods as just so much edubabble? Are there any new challenges for you in the classroom? Are you still able and willing to challenge the kids?

Are you letting a responsible student do too much of your work, like taking attendance and figuring grades? Do you give fewer assignments because you don't want to grade them? Are you spending more time in the teachers' lounge lounging than working?

Are you bored? If so, chances are you're boring, too.

Are you more easily frustrated than you used to be? More impatient? Less tolerant? Have you lost that most sustaining of qualities—your sense of humor?

Are you starting to believe there's no hope for this generation? Have you stopped believing that you make a difference? Have you quit trying to reach each and every kid?

Are you just there for the paycheck?

Most important, where is your heart? Is it still wide open to each and every student? Don't answer that too quickly. There's a difference between wholehearted passion and just marking time.

And this is about passion, not age. You can teach until you're ninety if your passion is still obvious to the kids.

Because just as they sensed your fear as a rookie, they sense your apathy now. And that's why you must leave; apathy breeds apathy.

I know it's scary—you've lived by the school calendar your whole entire life and you're wondering what you will be if you're no longer a teacher. Trust me on this, though. You'll always be a teacher at heart.

If you see yourself here, turn in your retirement papers.
Sometimes there's more valor in leaving than in staying.

It's Not a Job, It's a Calling

Dear Jamie,

You wrote asking my advice about a career in education. I'll answer you as honestly as I can.

I loved teaching. I did not leave education because I was down on kids. The kids were fine. I felt privileged to know most of them, and honored to play even a small role in their development. In fact, I'm still in touch with many of them and consider them friends. No, I left education because the job was consuming me. I was burned out and there are no resources for burned-out teachers.

So what caused the burnout? What eventually wore me down was the number of people I had to answer to—the kids, their parents, administrators, politicians. I always felt that with fewer students I could have been extraordinary, but the masses overwhelmed me.

I'm a type A perfectionist, but there is no perfect in education. It's a murky, blurry business, and you rarely know for sure that you've done it right. Each child is unique and has different needs. There's not enough time in the day, though, to figure out who needs what, and to meet all of those needs, which left me feeling inadequate a lot of the time.

You should not choose to teach because you "get summers off." That may have been true in the past, but it's not any longer. If you teach, the rest of your summers will be filled with workshops and classes to maintain your certification.

It's important that you really know yourself and what working conditions you need to thrive. As a teacher you will rarely be alone or have quiet, contemplative time. You must be physically strong and healthy because the pace is relentless—on your feet projecting your voice all day. You must be a master of organization and have a high tolerance for repetition. But if you teach, your coworkers will be some of the most highly principled people you'll ever meet in your life.

Most of what you need to be a good teacher can be learned, much from experience. But some inherent personality traits will allow you to flourish in the classroom, such as a sincere love of people, patience, optimism, and a good sense of humor. You cannot be thin-skinned or in constant need of approval. If there's a bit of the performer in you, if you relish being a role model, if you can easily handle not only volumes of paperwork but also volumes of people, then life in the classroom is for you.

And that lightbulb moment that teachers talk about? That moment when a kid really gets it? That is truly pure and splendid and can make all the rest worthwhile.

Teaching is not just a job. It's a calling. You can't do it any way but wholeheartedly.

So, Jamie, if you're thinking about teaching, perhaps the universe is trying to tell you something. Teach, because you were born to. It's a noble and honorable profession.

As for me, would I do it all again?

Absolutely.

CHAPTER 2

The Classroom Experience
YOU COULDN'T MAKE THIS STUFF UP

To Teach, With Love

Old habits die hard.

Which is why I found myself in front of the VCR on Labor Day, watching the 1966 film *To Sir, With Love* for the eighteenth time. As part of my annual back-to-school ritual I watched this movie, year after year, in search of the answer to that most perplexing question: how do you make students like and respect you, without simply giving in to their demands?

Because that's what it takes to be a truly great teacher. The kids need to like and respect you. Even the most difficult kid will try for a teacher he likes, and a good student can be turned off by a teacher she doesn't.

Though set in the 1960s the story is timeless. Mouthy, insolent, yet compelling teens test a new teacher, almost to the breaking point. The very human teacher has a eureka moment, takes back control of his classroom, and eventually wins his students' respect, and their hearts.

The story is timeless because learning is timeless. Trends in education come and go, legislation changes, and technology advances, but learning almost always boils down to the relationship between the student and the teacher.

A gifted teacher can teach a child to read using a stick in the dirt and the backyard as his classroom. But an antagonistic teacher can have every possible resource at his disposal, and still never reach a child.

At the end of the movie as Lulu sings the theme song, the students present Thackeray (Sidney Poitier) with a gift; he changes his mind and decides to stay in education after all, and once again I reach for the Kleenex.

In reality, though, those crystallizing moments for teachers are pretty few and far between. Oh, we have lots of one-on-one successes, poignant moments when we really connect with a student.

But rarely are kids organized enough to make cinematic drama. Just before he retired, though, my husband was lucky enough to experience an almost-movie moment.

He taught Advanced Placement (AP) history to sophomores. The classes were small, the students smart, spirited, motivated, and curious. So curious, in fact, that in one particular class a student named Maria started every single session by dropping into her seat and asking enthusiastically, "So, what are we going to learn today, Teach?" It was one of those rare groups where everyone clicked and the chemistry hummed. It was a teacher's dream come true.

Fast forward two years, and those students are now seniors, just sprung from high school forever. It's a hot June day, and he's teaching his current AP class of sophomores. The door opens. Silently, the entire AP class from two years before files into the room and sits down in the front two rows.

The sophomores gaped, awed.

"So, what are we going to learn today, Teach?" Maria asked.

And though their time as students at our school was over, those seniors stayed, all hour, to listen to his lesson.

Pass the Kleenex, please.

The Essence of Teaching and Learning—Zing!

When I graduated from college I had some pretty pie-in-the-sky ideas about what education was all about.

I thought it was about me delivering lively, fun lessons to students who would hang on my every word.

My mother told me I was born to teach, and in the beginning, it certainly felt as if that were true. On payday Fridays I would sail through the main office and my principal would say, "Kelly, you forgot to pick up your check again."

"You mean you *pay* me to do this?!" I would gleefully respond.

I soon realized, however, that my vision of myself teaching the elements of a short story to a bunch of spellbound teenagers didn't happen as effortlessly as I thought it would.

But why?

After all, I'd had all these education classes that taught me to design lessons and create teaching materials. No one made me take classes in being a social worker, nurse, psychologist, parent, or cop. I didn't know that when I got my teaching certificate I would be given all of these hats, and that I would have to wear them all at once.

Naively, I thought that I would teach and kids would learn. No one ever told me how many kids would not want to learn, either.

And that's what causes many teachers to burn out.

But there's one lucky group of teachers who never seem to lose their spark. They teach the Advanced Placement (AP) classes, the classes that count for college credit if the student passes the College Board test at the end of the year.

AP teachers are often veteran teachers, but there's an awesome fire still burning in their eyes, even if it is late in their careers.

What keeps that fire going? The answer is simple. AP teachers get to experience the true essence of teaching and learning, every single day.

Here's the equation: Take one teacher with a passion for her subject. Add students who love to learn.

The result? The essence of teaching and learning, where success is the only possible solution because the participants make it easy for each other.

In education we call it the "teachable moment," that moment when Jupiter aligns with Mars, everything falls into place, teachers teach and kids learn, effortlessly.

It's that *Zing*! you feel when you hit the sweet spot on a tennis racket.

It's as exhilarating as a runner's high, and you feel as though you could teach forever.

And it's why we became teachers in the first place, that thrill of teaching something we love to someone who is eager to learn it.

But too often it feels as though your running shoes are filled with lead because kids come to the equation with so many problems. Mental, physical, and emotional abuse. Parents who don't value education. Poverty. Substance abuse, either by the parents, the student, or both. Mental illness. Physical illness. Criminal records. Kids who come from homes that have no reading material whatsoever.

Teachers often wade through muck so deep that they are thrilled simply to get every student on task, let alone to hit that stride where the teaching and learning happens effortlessly and the participants make it easy for each other.

That's what smothers the fire, that sense of having to do so many things that you can't do any of them really well.

And that's why AP teachers still feel the fire. Because every single day, they get to hit the sweet spot on the tennis racket.

Zing!

A Good Sub Is Hard to Find

I stepped up to the podium and raised the baton. The students raised their instruments and—a few notes of lovely music segued into an ear-piercing screech and then—abrupt silence. Forty-two bug-eyed students looked at me in amazement.

Okay, so now I know. When band directors wave those skinny batons they are not just keeping time to the music. It's actually a highly nuanced set of directions for the musicians to follow.

In my defense let me just say this: I was twenty-three years old, just out of college, and had no music background whatsoever.

I was also substitute teaching for the first time. My delight at being assigned to a music class quickly turned into a good laugh at myself when I realized that I had no idea what I was doing.

I faired a bit better in the automotive class the next week. In my dress and high heels I sat on a grubby garage chair and chatted with a genial group of boys in dirty coveralls, while they puttered about with tools.

Such is the plight of the substitute teacher. It's not a job for those who can't think on their feet or go with the flow. The telephone becomes your alarm clock and the calls from sleepy secretaries start at 5 a.m. A last minute call can mean a harrowing drive across town to get to the school on time.

In a perfect world every sub is a certified teacher assigned to a class in his or her major. But that almost never happens. Most often subs are not certified teachers at all, but merely warm bodies with enough college credits and a clean background check to allow them to sub in a public school.

Unfortunately, a major in math is usually less important than a major in student discipline. When kids walk past a classroom and see a sub in place of their teacher, news travels fast and the high jinks begin.

All schools have a few subs that are so good teachers clamor to get them. These subs know the clientele, understand the culture, and make every effort to fit in.

But let's face it; sometimes, you really do get what you pay for. Low pay and the transient nature of the job can result in the arrival of some highly interesting characters.

At my school we once had a sub who left his class unattended. Our principal went to the classroom and waited. The sub showed up fifteen minutes later carrying a steaming Burger King bag

We never saw him again.

It's Hard to Describe the Impression I Made

All I wanted was to make a really good impression.

After all, I hadn't set foot in my alma mater since graduation on the football field that sweltering day in June 1976.

Just out of college, teaching jobs scarce, I did what we all did hoping to get a foot in the door—I registered for the worst job ever: substitute teaching. And finally, I got The Call: an assignment at good old Lake Fenton High School (LFHS).

I donned my best new grown-up clothes and took off in my beat-up Mustang. Zipping along, Diana Ross and I sang, getting pumped to face a room full of teenagers.

So lusty was our duet that I didn't hear the siren right away. I didn't notice the red and blue bubble lights flashing behind me, either. And when I did, unfortunately, we were right in front of the school. So naturally, the officer waved me into the parking lot, and pulled in behind me.

Shaking with nerves, I stoically endured the lecture about speeding (ten over), silently willing the officer to just hurry up and go away.

Notified of the fact that there was a police car in his school parking lot, of course the principal came out to investigate—and meet me for the first time.

Just when I thought it couldn't get any worse—I mean really—I looked up to see every classroom window filled with pointing, laughing students.

Red-faced and sweaty, I hustled in, got my schedule, and settled into first hour. It was a well-organized business class and the kids were on automatic pilot, giving me a minute to calm down.

I strolled along, looking over kids' shoulders, when I came upon something that brought the red flooding right back to my face. A young man had a condom on his desk—really quite shocking in 1981 when condoms weren't out of the closet yet. Worse, he was calmly unrolling it. Now what?! Take it away from him? (Yuck!) Or tell him to put it away? I opted for the latter.

Eventually, blissfully, it was lunchtime. I entered the only room I'd never been in at LFHS: the teachers' lounge. I felt every bit of my youth and inexperience as I sat with my former teachers in that forbidden, mysterious place.

"So, you're subbing for Mrs. Smith," said one teacher. "That's funny, I don't remember ever seeing her in here at lunch."

The full implication of that didn't register right away.

"What do you mean you never see Mrs. Smith in here during this lunch? Are you saying she doesn't have this lunch?" asked another teacher.

"You know, I don't think she does," she replied.

Holy crap. The secretary had incorrectly written out my schedule and somewhere in this building was a lunch-sprung group of unsupervised teenagers. I dropped my sandwich and bolted.

When I burst through the classroom door I came face-to-face with my hard-to-impress seventeen-year-old sister.

She just rolled her eyes.

Which pretty much summed up the impression I made that day.

Sniffle, Snort, Just Use Your Sleeve

Why is it that every high school kid's book bag holds an iPod, a cell phone, and a 20-ounce Coke, but no Kleenex?

Things get ugly fast during cold and flu season in public schools, because there's never enough Kleenex to go around. That means teachers spend their own money to supply them. They have to. It's either that, or fight the gag reflex all day listening to kids snork it up.

Seems like a small thing, doesn't it?

"Gee whiz, what's the big deal, it's only a Kleenex! Give the kid a Kleenex if he needs it!"

But it gets expensive. My classes used to go through about a box a week. Even if I bought the scratchy cheapies, it was about a buck a box. Multiply that by approximately thirty-eight weeks, and I was spending $38 a year on classroom Kleenex. My husband taught just down the hall, so between the two of us we were spending at least $76 a year. Multiply that by twenty years and, well, my stock portfolio could certainly look better.

Most districts purchase some tissue, but they usually run out before the first marking period is over. If the district supplied enough Kleenex for everyone all year long, there probably wouldn't be enough money left for textbooks.

Some teachers get creative, though. One guy I know swipes a roll of toilet paper from the bathroom to put on his desk. Another one provides a stack of rough brown industrial paper towels from the dispenser in the teachers' lounge. Some choose to ignore the wishes of their building principals and take the time to write passes to the bathroom all day, creating a lot of unsupervised hall traffic.

Some don't do anything. No Kleenex, no passes, nothing but your sleeve, kid.

Some students wouldn't use Kleenex even if they had them. Take Elliott for example. (Not his real name, for reasons that will become obvious.) This freshman sat in the back of my classroom every day for a year with his fingers up his nose to the knuckles. When he finally got what he was after, he ate it.

I kid you not.

So you have a building full of kids and a serious Kleenex shortage.

Now take all of the soap out of the bathrooms. High school bathrooms never have soap or paper towels, because after a few bad apples repeatedly dump the soap out of the dispensers and stuff the toilets with paper towels, the custodians get fed up and quit restocking them. In all my years as a student newspaper adviser, the number one letters to the editor complaint from the student body, year after year after year, was the state of the student bathrooms.

So the kids can't wash their hands and the germs have a free-for-all on every doorknob in the place. They're positively greasy. Every desk, every locker, every surface in a school building is just creepy-crawly with ick.

If you put the Kleenex on your desk so you can monitor your supply, you face a steady stream of kids coming up to honk in your face. All day. If you move the Kleenex away from desk, they stuff their pockets with enough tissues to get them through the day, further depleting your meager provisions.

But a little old gray-haired career teacher shared her tissue trick with me when I was student teaching. When a student asked her for a Kleenex she would rummage around in her purse for a minute, then finally pull out a wrinkled, wadded-up tissue. She would sort of shake it out and hand it to the kid and say, "Here. I'm pretty sure it's clean."

They never asked again.

I Could Really Use a Secretary Here

Brrring!

"Okay, class, that was the tardy bell. We'll begin discussing the Progressive Era right after I take attendance. Open your books to chapter 19 . . . I'll just enter this into the attendance book for the State . . . and then enter it into the computer for the office . . . okay, all set. Now . . ."

"Yo, Ms. Flynn, I know I'm late, but honest, it wasn't my fault."

"Antwan, this is your fourth tardy. I don't have a choice, the Student Handbook clearly states that students are to be referred to the office on the fourth tardy. Wait while I write up this discipline referral . . . there. Take this and go to the office. Okay, class, as you know, the Progressive Era took place in . . . oops, I almost forgot, Bobby and Joe, you need to sign the athletic eligibility to acknowledge that I verbally told you that you are ineligible to play this week. Sign right here. Okay, where were we? Ah yes, the Progressive Era . . ."

"Ms. Flynn, I need this field trip permission slip signed."

"Trina, I already signed your permission slip."

"I know, I know, but I lost that one and I had to get a new one. *Pleeease*, sign it so I can go?!"

"Later, Trina. We're in the middle of class here. Okay, when you read the chapter on the Progressive Era you learned . . ."

Knockknockknock.

"Ms. Flynn, I'm going home sick and my mom's on her way to pick me up. The lady in the office told me to go see all of my teachers and get my homework."

"Sally, I'm in the middle of class here."

"But I need my work *now*. My mom won't have the car later to come up and get it."

"Okay, just a minute. Class, start the questions at the end of the chapter. Okay, Sally, here you go. Now. Who can tell me what the Progressive Era . . ."

Knockknockknock.

"Ms. Flynn, the principal would like to see Josh White in his office right away."

"Josh, they need you in the office . . . Okay, where were we?"

"Ms. Flynn, what did we do last week? I was in Florida."

"Alex, you'll have to see me after class, we're in the middle of . . ."

"I don't got *time* after class, I got to get all the way upstairs to math class after this!"

"I'll talk to you at the end of the hour, Alex. Now, where were we?"

"MAY I HAVE YOUR ATTENTION. MAY I HAVE YOUR ATTENTION, PLEASE, FOR A VERY IMPORTANT ANNOUNCEMENT.

"Shhhh, class, listen, this sounds important."

"STUDENTS WHO ARE GOING ON THE HUMANITIES FIELD TRIP NEED TO REPORT TO THE FLAGPOLE IMMEDIATELY. I REPEAT, STUDENTS WHO ARE GOING ON THE HUMANITIES FIELD TRIP NEED TO REPORT TO THE FLAGPOLE IMMEDIATELY."

"Okay, if you're going on that field trip raise your hand so I can find your name on this list. When I find your name you may leave. Okay, done. Now, let's get down to work . . ."

"Hey, Ms. Flynn, you know I got, like, permission to leave early, right, 'cause we got, like, this cross-country meet today and the team gots to be on the bus by 1:30. You got the notice on that, right?"

"Let me just check the list, Bobby, and make sure you're on it. Yep, you can leave at 1:30."

Knockknockknock.

"Ms. Flynn, would you please pass out these overdue library slips to the appropriate students right away?"

"Oh, right. Here you go. Okay, class, what did you learn about the Progressive Era?"

Brrring!

Sigh.

Some days the lesson just gets lost in the paperwork.

Fasten Your Seat Belts!

"This isn't Disney World, people! These aren't bumper cars! I want to see six car lengths between you!"

Welcome to The Range, where driver's education students perfect skills like lane changes and backing up. I spent the day with Mr. Brave and Mr. Calm, two intrepid driver's training instructors who soothe students' giddy nerves with the antics of a good cop/bad cop comedy team.

Mr. Brave begins the lesson by walking students over the course on foot. They follow like puppies, nearly piling up Three Stooges style when he stops. He could tell them to yodel and they would, so eager are they to please this man who holds the key to freedom. Every one becomes a model student, including the ones who spent most of the year in detention.

With warm-hearted exasperation Mr. Brave hollers through his bullhorn a mix of encouragement and skepticism as students attempt a serpentine around cones—going backward.

"*No! No! No!*" he yells, shaking his head, hand smacking his forehead. "Jeezopeets, what the heck was *that?*" he mutters as a car backs squarely over a cone, tearing it in half.

It's *hot* on the range, over an acre of asphalt throbbing in the heat of a relentless sun. The sweating instructors are on high alert every minute, preaching safety, trotting miles alongside cars, giving instructions through the open window to the white-knuckled students behind the wheel.

I joined Mr. Calm and two students for their road debut. Everything that seems so charmingly comical on the range—herky-jerky stops, jackrabbit starts, and close turns around orange cones that drop like bowling pins—is terribly unnerving on a real road with real traffic.

With the serene, reassuring tone of a chatty airline pilot, Mr. Calm keeps up a steady stream of instruction and encouragement, even during the rather hair-raising passing of a tractor. Fortunately, I'm tucked into the back seat where I can't see much over a headrest the size of a mattress. I have a perfect view of the steering wheel, however, and a clear shot every time Mr. Calm's hand shoots out to grab it and guide us back onto the pavement.

While ninety minutes probably flew by for the students, I can't say the same for me. But by the end of the lesson both drivers are visibly more comfortable behind the wheel.

As I head home I think about all of the driving skills adults take for granted, like being able to talk and maintain speed at the same time, or stop at a stop sign and not ten yards short of it. Or simply, keeping the car between the lines.

But mostly, I marvel at those instructors, who think not a thing about getting into a fast car on a busy road with an adolescent kid who has yet to clip his first mailbox.

And I know one thing. It's not a job for sissies.

A Wing and a Prayer

Of course there's prayer in school.

One year, I prayed every single day before third hour. Fervently.

Because sometimes, luck of the draw in scheduling stacks classes with an assortment of students so disinterested in learning that you wonder why they bother to show up at all.

Every teacher has experienced it. For me, that freshman English class was a challenge from the first day in September to the last day in June.

I can close my eyes and picture them: the girls with their makeup, mirrors held high, inspecting their pores, adding yet more eye liner where there's already too much, an arsenal of beauty products spread out on their desks where their schoolbooks should be.

Those girls chattering furiously, and—I'm sorry—stupidly, about some boy who cheated on a friend, electrified by the juicy details of that morning's confrontation. Unwillingly my mind fast-forwards to the same girls as women, still obsessed with trashy gossip, the setting a bar instead of a classroom. Their faces are already settling into hard lines in hard makeup. They don't take kindly to having to shelve their conversation until class is over.

The boys are quiet, but it's a quiet born of apathy rather than good behavior. They sit and stare, dazed, eyes glazed, mouths open, not daydreaming exactly, but rather drugged looking.

One boy in particular shuffles in with pants hung low, empty hands shoved deep into the pockets of a dirty hoodie. No backpack, no textbook, no paper, no pencil—no pretext of learning at all. He slouches into his seat, drops his head, and flops his hood over his face. Less than a minute later drool starts to puddle on his desk.

I gaze at this class and not one single student appears to have come to class to learn. As proof of this the tardy bell rings and the kids continue unfazed, talking, laughing, gossiping, sleeping, staring. The bell is meaningless to them.

I won't lie to you. A class like this can wither the spirits of the best teacher. If you let them, teenagers will make you feel incidental, irrelevant, insignificant. You're a nuisance, an interloper, an imposition. It takes an incredible strength of will to stand up to that every day.

Really, truly, I don't know whether to laugh or to cry. This group is so unfocused, so *not* ready to learn, that I want to put my own head down on my desk.

But I don't. I say a silent amen, take a deep breath, and move forward, between the rows. A tap on a desk here, a murmur there, whispering names, making eye contact, connecting.

"Okay," I say. "Let's begin. . . ."

I Know Teachers Don't Live Under Their Desks, But . . .

I was sixteen years old, driving down Leroy Street in my hometown of Fenton, Michigan, when I passed Mrs. Lemere, my teacher, driving the other way.

I nearly drove off the road.

I had never seen a teacher outside of school. I don't know what I thought—I mean, I knew teachers didn't live at school. But I didn't imagine that they drove around in little blue Ford Pintos, either.

The age of discovery is different for all of us, but it's a nearly universal experience to learn—with surprise—that your teacher is human.

Some teachers go to great lengths to hide their humanity, believing that mystery breeds respect. They present themselves as teacher, and nothing but.

Others give students a highly orchestrated peek into their lives, building a persona around past football prowess or the fact that they drive a Harley. They know that if they plant the seed, the legend will grow.

And some go out of their way to be as accessible as possible, because you just never know what might build a bridge to a student. They share their lives freely, telling stories about their children, pets, hobbies, and vacations, always looking for a connection.

Sometimes, oddly enough, that personal stuff is the only memory a child takes from your class. I remember nothing about first grade, except the time my teacher, Miss Remington, brought her fancy new party dress to class on a hanger, and told us all about her impending dinner date with a new man. We were fascinated. I remember the exact look on my mom's face, too, when I relayed the story to her that afternoon.

A close encounter outside of school can be unsettling to student and teacher alike. I still squirm when I remember the time I ran into one of my students on a beach in upper Michigan. I was young, my bikini was small, and that poor seventh grader nearly got eyeball whiplash trying to look anywhere but at me.

Another time I came out of a bathroom stall in a local nightclub, and found one of my tenth graders primping at the mirror. I don't know whose gasp was louder, but hers included a frantic "Oh my God, please, don't tell my mom!"

It's a fine line we teachers walk. We know that if our students see another side of us, separate from the one that nags them to put their name on their paper, it can for some reason be the spark that makes them like us, which in turn makes them remember to put their name on their paper.

That's the thing about education: when you get right down to it, it's more about people—good, bad, silly, indifferent, flawed, funny, ordinary people—than anything else.

Am I On Candid Camera?

I'm sure glad I got out of education before the whole webcam and cell phone camera craze started. The thought of my classroom humiliations being caught on tape is just too mortifying.

No, I don't have anything to hide. My teaching skills were fine. It's just that teaching is a humbling experience. Teenagers womp on your self-esteem and dignity daily.

Black, glassy Orwellian eyes mounted in the ceiling supposedly curb misbehavior and increase security. But my tattered teaching ego sure wouldn't need to have my foibles immortalized for all eternity. I don't need some guy in Security replaying my webcam footage in slow motion for lunchtime entertainment, either.

In college, my teaching vision featured me, calm and poised, in front of students, spellbound and mesmerized. I would be serene. In control. Revered.

The reality fell far short of that. Whenever I started to pat myself on the back, something would happen to give my self-confidence a good, hard shake.

My first brush with reality occurred the very first week of my very first year of teaching, long before I grew eyes in the back of my head.

I was sitting at my desk, proudly surveying my domain. My students were taking a test. Except for the slight sound of pen on paper, the room was silent. Heads down, busy, quiet, concentrating. "Ah," I thought. "This is good. Very good." I smiled. I began grading papers at my desk.

Bonk.

Out of nowhere, a paper airplane sailed through the air with the precision of a Patriot missile and scored a direct hit—square on my nose. My head snapped up. My eyes popped in disbelief.

A fast look around the room revealed—nothing. Every single student had head bent to paper, diligently working.

My eyes narrowed to slits. I stared and waited. They kept working.

Carefully I looked at each student, certain that I would see a smirk, a smile, a raised eyebrow.

I watched. I waited.

Nothing. Everyone kept working.

How the culprit kept a straight face, I'll never know. And he's still out there, somewhere. A webcam would have caught him, but it would have caught the airplane bouncing off my nose, too. Uh, no thank you.

My next brush with reality was even more embarrassing. I was sitting at my desk, a line of students waiting to go over their writing assignments. One by one I talked to them, quickly and competently dispensing advice and information. I was feeling good. Capable. Efficient.

I leaned back in my chair to look up at a particularly tall kid.

Crrrr-ack!

Suddenly I was flat on my back, like a dying bug, legs waving in the air. My chair had snapped right off of its wheeled base. The entire chair fell backward, with me in it. My arms were even still on the armrests.

I lay there—astounded—looking up at this really tall kid who was suddenly even taller. The kid, bless his heart, hadn't even blinked. So intent was he on getting his question answered that he simply stepped to where he could see me better and earnestly talked on.

Perhaps this was just another of the inexplicable actions of the adults in his life. It didn't even register with him that I was no longer upright.

The bug-eyed kids in line behind him snorted with laughter. So funny was the sight of their teacher on her back with her feet in the air that it didn't occur to a single one of them to help me and my pride get up.

On second thought, maybe webcams aren't such a bad idea. Schools could compile the funny clips and produce a video.

Might start a whole new trend in fundraising.

As Safe at School as Anywhere

One winter day a year after the Columbine massacre, I was teaching my fourth hour class, when one of my students pointed out the window and yelled, "Hey look! It's a bum!"

I looked and, sure enough, right outside my classroom window was a scruffy man wearing a ragged coat, carrying a lumpy brown paper bag.

Immediately half the kids jumped up and headed for the window, laughing and pointing as if he were a circus act.

I processed the information from a different point of view:

"Dirty scruffy guy, don't know who he is, never saw him before, what's he got in the bag, danger, danger, DANGER!"

"Get away from that window this minute!" I hissed. "Get over by the door right now!"

Every kid froze, shocked by my tone of voice.

I called the office, keeping my eye on the guy and the kids. Eventually, Security arrived (though not nearly fast enough for me). It turned out that he was, indeed, a homeless man.

My students forgot the incident as quickly as it happened.

I didn't.

Over the next few days I thought a lot about "What if . . ."

What if he had a gun? What if he had a bomb? What if, what if, *what if*?

It's a testament to our optimism that school districts aren't turning their buildings into prisons to make them safer. No one really thinks another Columbine will happen.

But it's important in times of crisis to feel like you're doing something, anything. So, with limited budgets, schools have done what they could.

One cheap and easy step toward peace of mind was to issue identification badges to staff members. But how effective are they, really? Even in a large school most staff members recognize each other, even if they don't know each other by name.

Most schools started locking all outside doors except one. They were careful about it at first, too. But gradually, the fear recedes and we get lax. Doors are left open and untended. Today it's the door where the food is delivered. Tomorrow it's the loading dock. The next day Johnny sticks a rock in the door to leave it open for his friend.

Nonschool personnel walk in and out of schools all day. Signs posted on the doors encourage visitors to check in at the office, and the good and honest people gladly do. Someone intent on doing harm will, of course, ignore them.

We know that smaller buildings and smaller student populations allow us to keep better tabs on things, yet the trend for upsizing buildings continues. And in a large building with a large student population, there are literally dozens and dozens of places to hide—people or things.

Surveillance cameras may be helpful, but would they have helped at Columbine? No. Dylan Klebold and Eric Harris were intent on a grand massacre and were willing to die in the process. What would they care about a videotape?

Lockdown drills accustom kids to the idea of huddling on the floor under a table or behind a filing cabinet.

But the TV generation can imagine every possible scenario: "Ms. Flynn, what if the guy comes through the window, not the door? What if they're already hiding in your back room and we don't know it and we're locked in with him? What if he just shoots the lock off?" the kids ask.

I don't have the answers.

Like it or not our security—in schools and in society—is not necessarily something we can assure, regardless of what Michael Chertoff or your local superintendent tells you.

So are schools any more secure today than they were before Columbine?

Yes.

About as secure as our borders and airports since 9/11.

And that's not exactly comforting.

We All Want Those Teachers Gone

True story: I once was evaluated on the very last day of school in June. The very last day! And then I wasn't formally evaluated again until eight years later.

I wasn't complaining. For perfectionist me, evaluations were always nerve-racking, sweat-generating, panic-producing experiences. I was happy to slide under the radar.

I like to think that so much time passed between evaluations because I was such a top-notch teacher. I'm sure my superiors knew I had things under control from casual observation, or from passing by my open classroom door. They didn't need to be in my classroom to know that I handled all my own discipline, kept good records, and turned my grades in on time. Perhaps they heard good things from my students and their parents.

After all, any good administrator has a finger on the pulse of the building and knows the strengths and weaknesses of the staff. And besides, I knew a teacher who didn't cut it and got fired, so I knew they were evaluating somebody, if not me.

So I was surprised when someone grumbled to me recently, "Oh, those unions. Once those bad teachers get tenure they can never be fired."

That persistent, yet false assumption is not true. Tenure is not a job guarantee. Tenure laws clearly outline procedures that allow school administrators to fire incompetent teachers, whether they have tenure or not.

Too often, though, where the system breaks down is in the evaluation process. Evaluations take time. Documentation is required. But money shortfalls mean administrative staffs get cut, and remaining administrators are spread too thin. When time is tight, time-consuming teacher evaluations might fall to the bottom of the list—which is probably what happened with my last-day-of-school evaluation. The busy principal forgot, then rushed to do it at the last minute to meet a quota.

Also, people who work in schools tend to be . . . well . . . nice. They're caretakers. They don't want to hurt anyone's feelings. Administrators may be understandably reluctant to use the process on a senior teacher who may be an old friend, someone they came up through the ranks with. So maybe they look the other way and hope that teacher retires soon.

On my staff we all knew who the "bad" teachers were, and we wanted them gone. They reflected badly on all of us. And we'd speculate among ourselves about why administrators didn't get tough and just evaluate them out of the system.

Many administrators have chosen to concentrate on the new crop of teachers coming in. Determined not to make any hiring mistakes, they've beefed up the evaluation process on nontenured teachers, and don't keep the ones who don't cut it.

It's also important to note that when done well, the evaluation process can help a so-so teacher improve.

That's the thing, though; the process is only as good as the people who use it.

CHAPTER 3

Seasons

IT TAKES NO MORE THAN A CHANGE IN THE WIND TO RILE THEM UP

Blackboard Jungle Bells

(Sung to the tune of "Jingle Bells")

Dashing through the halls, through the prevacation fray,
Kids racing to and fro, laughing all the way;
The noise makes my head throb, My God, I look a fright,
What toil it is to "tame the beasts," this day to expedite.

Chorus
Starting bells, tardy bells, ring in the hallway!
O what grit one has to have to make it through this day.
Sugar high, caffeine buzz, what more can I say?
O what fun winter break will be, let's hear a big hooray!

Of course it had to snow, and complicate my plight,
I slipped and fell right on my tush much to the kids' delight.
Snowballs flying fast, shoes and coats all wet,
Kids caught up in being kids, gone is all etiquette.

A day or two ago, so close to this Yuletide,
The whole class had a cold, sniffling and red-eyed.
The Kleenex box ran dry, but Johnny's nose did not;
He got into a sneezing fit, and slimed my sleeve with snot.
(Chorus)

The kids just can't sit still, they know vacation's near;
Lessons are a bore to them this special time of year.
But teachers must push on, learning's the bottom line;
The struggle has exhausted me and it's only half past nine.
(Chorus)

The lunch buffet was grand, someone tried it all;
They pushed it to the max, now there's vomit in the hall.
The kids don't seem to mind, they all got quite a laugh;
The culprit was Mr. McGraw, a teacher on the staff.
(Chorus)

The kids have all pitched in, raised money for the poor;
You only have to watch them work to have your faith restored.
Gifts for a lonely child, and food for those in need;
In spite of what you generally hear their motive is not greed.
(Chorus)

Last hour's finally here, one more to make it through;
My feet and back do ache, but I'm not sad or blue.
The giggling smiles of kids, sustained me all day long;
They've piled my desk with candy canes, and courted me with song.
(Chorus)

At last the day is done, the kids burst forth with glee;
They race from the classroom, I dodge the stampede.
I flop down at my desk, and realize the truth,
One reason that I love to teach: the enthusiasm of youth!
(Chorus)

'Twas the Day before Break

'Twas the day before break, and all through the school,
Not a student was working, most behaving like fools.
DVDs were cued up, kids played learning games,
In hopes that the chaos could somewhat be tamed.

The children were buzzing from sugar and glee,
Anticipation mounting for the next two weeks free.
And I and my nerves, or what little was left,
Had finally sat down, bemused and bereft.

When out in the hall there arose such a clatter,
I sprang from my desk to see what was the matter.
Away to the door, thinking, "Oh God, what now?"
Threw it wide open, expecting a row.

The light from the window at the end of the hall,
Framed the silhouette of men, some short and some tall.
My wondering eyes saw a crazy sideshow,
A state politician with eight yes-men in tow.

With a perfect white smile so dazzling and slick,
I knew in a moment, this was political schtick.
Most rapid with handshakes, he cruised down the hall,
A publicity ploy was the gist of it all.

"Now, test scores, Now merit pay, Now vouchers for all!
Oh funding, Oh tax cuts, Oh budget shortfall.
I'll save education, I tell you, I will,
If you'll only help send me to Capitol Hill!"

As campaign leaflets before an election do fly,
The truth and straight answers were in short supply.
So up to the main office, the yes-men, they flew,
With an agenda of promises and the politician, too.

And then in a twinkling, I saw from afar,
The smiling glad-handing of the self-proclaimed star.
As I drew back my hand and was turning to hide,
Down the hall came the press corps with cameras held wide.

The Rep was all dressed in his suit and matched tie,
This orchestrated photo op would not pass him by.
A bundle of laptops he had flung on his back,
And he looked like a fence just opening his pack.

His eyes, how they scanned each one for approval,
Hecklers were targeted for early removal.
His droll little mouth which spoke only swill,
Begged our support for his education bill.

"Per pupil funding must be slashed," so he said.
"Big merit awards and laptops, you'll get instead.
So we cut adult ed., didn't need it anyhow,
But don't touch my salary, that's a sacred cow."

He preened and he postured, a self-righteous old elf,
And I gagged when I saw him in spite of myself.
A wink of his eye and a nod of his head,
Soon gave me to know I had everything to dread.

He spoke without stopping, full of rhetoric was he,
"The Report Cards are coming, failing schools cannot be!
I'll save education! The schools I can fix!
But input from teachers we'll just have to nix."

He sprang to his Town Car, to his cronies he waved,
And away they all sped, another school to be saved.
But I heard him exclaim, "Keep this in mind—
With me at the helm there's No Child Left Behind!"

Santa, Save Us

(Sung to the tune of "Jolly Old Saint Nicholas")

Jolly old Saint Nicholas
lean your ear this way.
Please come and save us from this
education fray.
Democrats are coming soon,
What will be their plan?
New, improved NCLB?
Will it just be canned?

States want enough funding to
meet requirements.
Please rescue local control
on how money's spent.
Industries like tutoring
and big testing, too,
Must be held accountable
for motives untrue.

Teachers, oh, so weary of
teaching to the test,
More than anything they want

reform that makes sense.
Veteran teachers told they're not
highly qualified,
Skills and years' experience
are just pushed aside.

Education can't be fixed
'til it's clearly seen.
Slanted studies from think tanks
spinning facts obscene.
Help us work together,
We don't need to spar.
Make government listen well,
See things as they are!

When NCLB is up,
Don't reauthorize.
It's not good for kids or schools,
It's a pack of lies.
All the answers that you need,
You will find in schools.
Tell big business to butt out,
Crooked Ed feds, too.

System is illogical,
Pols have too much clout.
Reform conversation leaves
educators out.
Work with us not against us,
That's the golden rule.
We are the experts on what
happens in our schools.

And while you're granting wishes,
Here are a few more.
Send us kids, well loved and fed;
Good homes, please restore.
Bobby's dad is in Iraq,
He would like him home.
Susie's mom can't pay the rent,
On the streets they roam.

Johnny's dad got busted for
selling dope again;
He won't be there for his boy
when he's in the pen.
Nellie cannot concentrate
because her folks fight;
She cannot get any sleep
'cause it's worse at night.

True learning is in danger,
It's no longer fun.
All this wicked drilling means
imagination's done.
Learning should be joyful, there's
more to life than tests.
Please don't let us down, Santa,
Pols don't know what's best!

Up On Capitol Hilltop

(Sung to the tune of "Up On the Rooftop")

Up on the hilltop,
Pols pass laws,
They act as if they're Santa Claus.
"Fixing" education
is their gift,
But true learning issues
get short shrift.

Ho, ho, ho!
Government's the foe!
Go, go, go!
Public schools to overthrow!
Up on the hilltop,
Slick, slick, slick,
Just one more
political gimmick.

First comes the NAEP test
for little Nell,
Joy of learning

gets death knell.
Give her a voucher
if her school fails,
Make her education
go retail.

Ho, ho, ho!
Testing woe!
Ho, ho, ho!
Another low blow!
Up on the hilltop,
Another dirty trick;
They have the answer,
Political schtick.
While your school crumbles,
They pass NCLB,
Then go on a
spending spree.
There's nothing left
for your funding needs,
Down go schools in
bankruptcy.

Low, low, low!
Tight politico!
Owe, owe, owe!
Funding no show!
Up on the hilltop,
They live high.
Money for schools
in short supply.

Whether an elephant
or an ass,
Corporate says "jump,"
And a law they'll pass.
They won't rest
'til they privatize it all;
True progress
they will stonewall.

Ho, ho, ho!
Quid pro quo!

Ho, ho, ho!
Follow the dough!
Up on the hilltop,
They bootlick.
Down thru' the ages,
Fool the public.

Pols need facts
to fit their goals,
Put their "experts"
on the payroll.
Lobbyists with kickbacks
have last word,
While educators
go unheard.

No, no, no!
Don't ask the pros.
Whoa, whoa, whoa!
The "trenches" don't know.
Up on the hilltop,
It's political gain;
Public education
down the drain!

NCLB: Over and Done Is What This Should Be

(Sung to the tune of "Over the River")

Over five years of dealing with
No Child Left Behind;
Its time is up, we've had enough,
Politicos don't be blind.

Over the tongue and through the lips,
"It's working" Bush does profess;
But the facts say no, too much woe,
NCLB is not a success.

Over the Hill and through chambers,
Legislative process is slow;
They orchestrate and negotiate,
But must fix this imbroglio.

Over one hurdle and to committee,
NCLB to reauthorize;
The language stinks, crooked ratfinks,
Education bastardized.

Pass committee and to the House,
NCLB will go;
Pols know the way to carry the day,
And repay corporate dough.

Over the people, straight to the boss,
Big favors to pay off;
Mr. CEO, political maestro,
Belly up to the trough.

Over phone lines and through the 'net,
Amendments they do fly;
Education rot is sold and bought,
As pols line up allies.

Onto the calendar, sit and wait,
While politicians jaw;
The work begun will not get done,
While they hem and haw.

Over the teachers and to hearings,
Duplicitous experts all;
They make up the stats, simply fat cats,
True reform to stonewall.

Across the country and in classrooms,
Teachers are informed;
Let educators be co-creators,
When education's reformed!

Over the days and through the night,
the government debates;

Mirrors and smoke, the data's a joke,
Yet policy they dictate.

Over the lips, into the mic,
Oh, how the hot air doth blow;
They preen and pose, folly exposed,
Yet ed. law they impose.

Turn over your test, bubble your sheet,
Student interest starts to wane;
"Tests are dumb and school's not fun,"
Pressure makes them complain.

Over five years and countless tests,
The kids have grown so weary;
Shrewd Uncle Sam, promoting a sham,
Turned education dreary.

Over and done is what this should be,
Please scrap the whole dang thing;
Start from scratch, don't try to patch,
Be more accommodating.

Over our wishes, behind closed doors,
The feds do as they wish;
The People must say, to Congress today,
Enough of this rubbish!

A Snow Day Is a Holiday

It was sixth hour. Snow had started falling heavily outside and Bob's eyes kept straying toward the clock. If this keeps up, he thought, there's no way we'll have school tomorrow. Suddenly, the PA system came on. Everyone froze, listening intently.

"MAY I HAVE YOUR ATTENTION, PLEASE. THE WEATHER SERVICE IS PRE-DICTING A SEVERE SNOWSTORM FOR TONIGHT. PLEASE LISTEN TO YOUR LO-CAL RADIO AND TELEVISION STATIONS IN THE EVENT THAT SCHOOL MAY BE CANCELED TOMORROW."

Yes!

Bob began gathering up his things. The bell rang and everyone burst into the hall, chattering excitedly.

When Bob got home he turned on the TV. Hmm . . . Nothing yet. Well, there was still time. He turned on the radio, too, just in case.

He went to the window and looked out. About three inches of snow covered the ground, and it was still coming down. He sat and watched.

He wondered about the test that was scheduled for tomorrow. He thought about doing his schoolwork, and wondered if he dared skip it. If he didn't have school tomorrow, he could get caught up then. Or not. Maybe he'd lie on the couch and watch TV all day. No doubt he'd have to shovel, but it was worth it if he didn't have school.

He went back to the TV and sat down. He watched the crawl across the bottom of the screen. Some evening activities and sporting events were canceled. No schools yet. He couldn't seem to pull his eyes away from that crawl.

After dinner, Bob went online and checked the list of school closings at the local TV station's website. The list was growing, but his school still wasn't there.

What if we're the only school that's not called off, he thought. It's happened before. Oh, that would be so disappointing.

He went back to the TV. Hmm. Maybe if he switched to another station.

Still nothing.

He watched the crawl for a while longer. He wondered which roads the superintendent drove when he went out to check them. He wondered what code word the superintendent used when he called the media to cancel school.

Feeling restless, he put on his boots and went outside.

He looked up and down the street. It was coming down so hard that the streetlight two blocks away was barely visible. No sign of a salt truck. No sign of a plow. Good. He took a few experimental steps in the snow. Then he ran and took an all-out slide across the driveway, skidding to a stop. All right, he thought. It's slippery under all that snow.

When he came in, Bob called his buddy Steve.

"Have you heard anything yet?" he asked.

"No, not yet," Steve said.

"Well, call me the minute you hear," Bob said.

"Okay, you do the same," Steve replied.

It grew late, and Bob knew he should get to bed or he'd be tired tomorrow. I'll just watch TV a few more minutes, he thought. He put the remote next to his bed in case he wanted to check in the night. He closed his eyes and tried to sleep.

Six hours later he awoke with a start, well before his alarm went off, and reached for the remote. He held his breath and counted to ten superstitiously. Okay, he thought, it's got to be there now. He turned on the TV and started reading the crawl, still holding his breath.

Yes! There it was! The first official snow day of the year!

Bob turned off the TV and burrowed back down into the covers.

And thanked God that he taught at a school that didn't require teachers to report on snow days.

The Wicked Week of Candy

If the incessant crinkling of candy wrappers doesn't make you crazy, the frenzy of the sugar-buzzed beasts will.

Yes, the wicked week of candy is frightful, the week when kids' backpacks bulge not with schoolbooks, but with Halloween loot, brought to school to share with some and with which to torture others.

First, teachers must survive Halloween and the delirious glee caused by costumes and trick-or-treat anticipation. But when Halloween is over, there's a new demon to deal with: the all-consuming preoccupation with the candy that is sneaked into the classroom.

Picture it: The class settles down and you start the lesson. They listen, rapt. Suddenly, the quiet is disrupted. *Crinklecrinklecrinkle.* It's the unmistakable sound of a candy wrapper (a sound, by the way, that can bring my dogs out of a sound sleep in another room). You look around for the culprit. So does everyone else. They want to know who's got what and, more important, will they share? As you look pointedly around the room, the candy sneaker freezes. The crinkling stops. You continue the lesson.

Soon, *crinklecrinklecrinkle.* You pretend not to hear it. *Crinklecrinklecrinkle.* Ah, ha! You spot him. Justin in the third row has a full-sized bag of Skittles, a candy of such undiluted sugar quality it's like a saccharine IV. Watching him eat one after another makes your fillings ache.

It's amazing. The sneaking of candy commands their attention, completely and utterly. The ones who brought candy are preoccupied with sneaking it out of their backpacks and into their mouths. The ones who didn't bring candy are preoccupied, too, watching the ones who did. You'd think world treaties were at stake the way the have-nots negotiate with the haves.

And so it continues, every hour, every day, until all the candy is gone. It's annoying beyond belief.

I know I wasn't alone in my temptation to give into it, to say, "Oh, what the heck. Go ahead, eat your candy. Eat it until you can't eat any more!" But then you picture thirty kids corked up on unlimited sugar and, fortunately, reason returns.

The coup de grace is that wrappers from the candy you never saw them eat are all over your classroom floor when they leave.

In desperation, I once came very close to becoming the scrooge (and the scourge) of my neighborhood. "I'm passing out pencils and pens for Halloween this year," I declared. "God knows they need them—more than half the class brings nothing to write with on any given day."

Fortunately for the kids (and probably our windows) my husband intervened. That, he said, is pushing the schoolmarm stereotype a bit too far.

A survey conducted by BIGresearch said that U.S. consumers spend about $3.29 billion on Halloween. On average, $18.07 a person is spent on sweets. And a whole lot of that ends up in classrooms.

Crinklecrinklecrinkle.

Mmmm . . . a Snickers mini.

If you can't beat 'em, join 'em.

Full Moons and Fridays

"MAY I HAVE YOUR ATTENTION, PLEASE. IF YOU ATE THE TOMATO SOUP AT LUNCH TODAY, PLEASE COME TO THE MAIN OFFICE IMMEDIATELY. I REPEAT, IF YOU ATE THE TOMATO SOUP AT LUNCH TODAY, PLEASE COME TO THE MAIN OFFICE IMMEDIATELY."

That announcement came over the PA system half way through sixth hour. After a moment of stunned silence, my class, and every other class in the building, exploded in laughter, the crescendo echoing down the halls. It was the single funniest thing that ever happened in my teaching career. It was a moment right out of *Porky's*, to be sure.

It was not so funny for the poor souls trudging in trepidation to the office. Turns out the principals got a tip that someone slipped Ex-Lax into the soup at lunch. Luckily, no one got sick, and we all had a good laugh at the absurdity of life in a school.

Of course it was a Friday. Everything odd happens on Friday. Fist fights, drug busts, bomb threats, pulled fire alarms, ranting parents, so many kids in trouble that it's standing room only in the main office—always on a Friday.

Every school has a rhythm, a flow, a certain feeling in the air when all is well. And the people who work there have a keen ability to sense when it's about to be disrupted. When disruption looms, the air crackles with expectation, putting teachers on high alert. They pass each other in the halls, eyebrows raised, whispering, "What's up? What's going on? Is there a full moon?" They watch their students more closely, peek into the hall more often, just a little more observant, a little more aware.

Because full moons and Fridays are when legends are born.

The time a freshman girl in my first hour class burst into tears, creating a weird chain reaction that caused every other girl to burst into tears, too—happened on a Friday. The time I found a thick braid of hair with the barrette still intact on my classroom floor after two freshmen girls were hauled off to the office for a truly feral fistfight—happened on a Friday. The time one of my students climbed out of my classroom window and into a car waiting at the curb—to the delight of passersby, no doubt—happened on a Friday.

Teachers are not immune, either. One time I looked out my classroom window to see a parent I had been trying to reach for days parked at the curb. I wanted to talk to her, but I knew she would be long gone by the time I got all the way down the hall and out the door. Imagine her surprise when she looked up to see the teacher from Room 102 come feet first out of the window and sprint across the lawn.

Yes, of course. It was Friday.

Summer, Sweaty Summer

Step inside, and the smelly, steamy heat slaps you like a wet sweat sock. To an unsuspecting visitor, it's disconcerting—even shocking. But those of us on the inside know that the first hot spell in late May turns schools into sweat boxes and students into zombies.

Sleepy, heavy-lidded, glazed and dazed students droop across their desks. Small classroom windows stand wide-open, letting in better-than-nothing air. Sans screens, they're an open invitation to equally somnolent bees, whose buzzing appearance jars kids into dramatic squeals of terror.

In desperation, teachers turn off classroom lights, hoping to bring down the temperature a degree or two, or at least give that impression. Some students fan themselves furiously, raising their temperature even more.

The groundskeeper zips by, open throttle, clad in headphones and sunglasses, tractor engine stunningly loud under the window, but bringing some relief with the fresh scent of cut grass. If your students don't have allergies you can leave the window open, and it's heaven.

There's no nice way to say it—the halls smell like people unfamiliar with deodorant or soap. You can't escape the smell, either: it's everywhere, imprinted in your nose, clinging to your clothes, making you self-conscious and eager to hurry home and peel it away, straight into the washer.

Wilted teachers make excuses to hang around in air-conditioned offices during their planning hours, where secretaries and principals cheerfully work, as fresh as they were upon arriving that morning.

It's a loose look teachers have adopted for the day, dressed for picnics rather than business: sandals, no socks, loose dresses, ponytails, even shorts, anything to catch a breath of breeze and release body heat.

In spite of the lethargy, tempers are short and flare easily. Shiny-faced kids move through too-crowded halls, sticky elbow bumping sticky elbow, clammy skin on skin.

Cranky with heat, students beg to go outside or just put their heads down and sleep. A few brave teachers do take them outside, while other classes watch jealously from the sauna windows. Some kids feign work for fear of being dragged back inside, but most don't, giving themselves over to cool grass and cooler shade.

After school, teachers run out and spend their own money on fans for their classrooms, then Sharpie their names all over them, hoping they won't disappear overnight because they're too big to be locked up in cabinets. The canned breeze is divine, in spite of the constant scramble to anchor papers on desks.

On these blistering days little work gets done, and the day feels pregnant with waiting. Unused to such discomfort, kids watch the clock, thinking of popsicles and pools and air-conditioning waiting at home, waiting for the last bell of the day, the last day of school.

The novelty of the heat wave wears off fast. Soon teachers scan the sky hopefully, looking for clouds, longing for rain.

There's work yet to be done before that last bell of the year.

CHAPTER 4

Students

WE LOVE THEM . . . WELL, MOST OF THEM . . . MOST OF THE TIME . . . REALLY

We All Failed Abdul

It was one of the most frustrating things I've ever experienced. I felt inadequate. Deficient. Neglectful. I failed, completely and utterly.

If I felt that way, I can only imagine how he felt.

Abdul came into my class speaking not one word of English. None, nada, zip, zilch (all words he didn't know).

We had no translator. No cue cards. No cheat sheets. This young man had been sent to a school where he could not communicate at all with the people around him. He couldn't ask for a Kleenex. He couldn't tell someone if he had a stomach ache. He couldn't even ask to go to the bathroom.

For an entire year Abdul and I lived in a world of pantomime, exaggerated gestures, dramatic facial expressions, using eyebrows to communicate—raised in question, scowling in misunderstanding. Because of cultural differences I dared not even pat his back in reassurance.

The county education service provided a tutor for Abdul—he got one, for one whole hour a week, to help in six classes. I couldn't even call his parents for a conference—they didn't speak English either. I doubt that they expected him to learn the content his classes offered, though. I think they hoped that he would learn English simply by being exposed to it for eight hours a day.

On September 11, 2001, the principal came on the PA system and told us to turn our classroom monitors to CNN. As we watched the horror unfold, one by one the students' eyes slid over to Abdul, back to the screen, then back to Abdul. I have no idea how much Abdul understood of what he saw on TV. But he didn't need English to read the cool speculation in the other students' eyes.

I was confounded by how to grade him. I taught English. My students were graded on how much they learned in English. He spoke no English. If I had eight hours to spend with Abdul every day, I could have taught him to read. But I didn't. I had twenty-six other students in that hour alone—twenty-six lively freshmen with a multitude of personalities and needs. I was busy every minute trying to keep them engaged and on task.

At the end of first marking period I could tell that Abdul was disappointed with his report card. His tutor, a kind man with warm brown eyes whose workload was as heavy as mine, told me that Abdul had earned the highest grades at his former school. I suspected as much—I could see the light of intelligence in Abdul's eyes.

I've often wondered what happened to Abdul. Did he go back to his home country? Did he have any pleasant memories at all of his time in the American public school?

I know one thing, though. I could have given Abdul a perfect example of irony, something we covered in that freshman English class.

He was eager to learn, but couldn't. Many of his American classmates could learn, but wouldn't.

I Am Not a Hero

From my teaching journal . . .

I am a rotten teacher.

I keep thinking that if I just try a little bit harder, if I'm kinder, more understanding, more creative, more *something*, I can fix things in my second hour.

Through the luck of the draw the kids in this class are all friends and neighbors who grew up together in the same trailer park. I gather from their conversations that they party together almost every night. They're only freshmen, but this partying includes booze. Lots of it.

Absenteeism is high. They aren't here to learn. They are here because it's something they have to get through until tonight's party.

This group is more tightly knit than George W.'s brow, and they follow one leader.

His name is Roberto and he wears enough gold around his neck to make the payment on my Suburban. He's like a four-foot, eight-inch Mafia don.

And every girl in the room is crazy about him.

His grade point average is about a 1.0, but to these freshman girls, he is a god. They baby him, mother him, lie for him, cover for him, and do his schoolwork for him. Women's lib has not reached their neighborhood.

I don't get it. All this little twerp has to do is snap his fingers and these girls jump to do his bidding. Apparently bad taste starts young. The boys worship him, too, because he gets the girls.

I think he's either hung over every day or on drugs. He puts his head down and is sound asleep immediately. When I wake him up (every day) he says he doesn't feel good and needs to call home and have someone bring him some medicine. I don't know how he manages that, though, because I've left messages at his house every day for a week and no one returns my calls.

Roberto and I struggled for a bit to see who was actually going to be in charge of this class. I won. But he fought the valiant fight, and now the rest of the class thinks they are punishing me for dethroning their king by not doing their classwork.

I am irrelevant to them. I'm this grown-up person who nags at them to pay attention, but I just don't have anything to offer that's as titillating as the sex, drugs, and rap 'n' roll that goes on in their lives once they leave this building.

If this were a movie I would be the hero and change the lives of every one of these kids.

I would be Sidney Poitier in *To Sir, With Love*.

I would be Michelle Pfeiffer in *Dangerous Minds*.

I would be Richard Dreyfuss in *Mr. Holland's Opus*.

In reality, I'm just an ordinary teacher. I want to light the fire of curiosity in their eyes, but I can't even find the matches.

I feel like I've tried everything, but in the fifty-five minutes that I have with them each day, I can't change a lifetime of habits learned at home.

They're all miffed because they think I'm picking on their precious Roberto. They've known him longer, they like him better, and he doesn't give them homework.

It's sad, but I don't know if I can turn it around. I think I'm going to have to let this one go. In movies teachers always end up doing miraculous things with boys like this. But this is not a movie.

And I am not a hero.

Sometimes you just have to let the Robertos of the class put their heads down and go to sleep.

Then you can concentrate on the ones who are awake.

Bad Apples Trash the Bathrooms

I answered the classroom phone and my principal said, "Kelly, have you got a photographer available down there?" I was the school newspaper adviser so the question wasn't unusual. The assignment, however, turned out to be anything but usual.

"Sure," I replied. "What's up?"

"Just send him down," he said. "Tell him to hurry."

An appalled student photographer returned a few minutes later. "I can't believe it," he said. "I had to take a picture of poop!"

Yep, a phantom duker had been hitting the boys' bathroom regularly, leaving his calling card in the middle of the floor. Administrators and custodians were at their wits' ends. The photo was evidence—for what, I'm not sure.

My apologies for the inelegance of that true story. But in all honesty, sometimes school is as strange as Alice's looking glass, mirroring the curiosities of the society we've created. Every teacher I know has stories of the bizarre but true.

I advised the student newspaper for eight years and the number one student complaint in letters to the editor, bar none, was the state of the student bathrooms. Clogged sinks and toilets, empty soap dispensers, and the lack of toilet paper or paper towels topped the list—on a good day.

On a bad day, it's beyond imagining. Vandalism. Graffiti. Destruction. One year an enterprising young student reporter decided to do an investigative piece on the bathrooms' cleanliness. She created a checklist and visited each school bathroom four times a day, documenting what she found.

It was revolting.

Some of the mess was accidental. Most was intentional. For example, the same thick squirt of salad dressing, from a packet pilfered from the cafeteria, stayed on a stall door for four days.

It's a complex problem. The bad apples trash the bathrooms, ruining them for everybody. Heroic custodians, fed up with mopping up soap that has been intentionally poured on the floor four days in a row, eventually quit filling the soap dispensers. If paper towels continue to be stuffed into toilets, they quit stocking those, too. If things get really bad, principals lock the least patrolled bathrooms.

Hall monitors do their best, but they can't be everywhere at once. When students badly outnumber the adults, it's easy to find places to act out—in defiance, anger, and ignorance.

Let me be clear about this: no school is exempt from student bathroom problems, no matter how nice the district. But the state of the student bathroom does seem to reflect the state of mind of the students who use it. What do you see driving down the street in certain parts of town? Vandalism. Graffiti. Destruction.

In California, students protested the quality of the bathrooms, resulting in state legislation requiring schools to maintain them.

Bathroom legislation? Talk about the curiosities of society. Wouldn't it be more effective if parents simply taught their kids better bathroom etiquette?

It lends a whole new meaning to the term "potty training."

Too Much Stuff

Before birthdays and holidays no doubt your teenagers hand over their lists. But before you go hog wild at the mall, take a moment and think about what you really want your child to have.

It's easy to buy a bunch of stuff that's going to break or go out of style. It is much more difficult to teach them the value of a dollar and the meaning of hard work.

Don't get me wrong. There's nothing wrong with having nice things. It's the *attitudes* about the things that can be a problem.

We teacher-types look for the lesson in everything. And the lesson we see being sent to many kids is that everything will be handed to you, everything is disposable, and if it you lose it, not to worry, we'll get you another one.

The message, of course, that we want to see given to our students, is that you get what you earn, and if you lose it, there will be consequences.

The halls and classrooms of a high school tell the story.

For example, in a high school, small change is, well, small change. Kids can't be bothered to pick it up.

I once stopped to pick up a nickel off the floor in the hall. One of my students happened to be walking behind me.

"Ms. Flynn!" she whispered. "I can't believe you picked that up! I'm *sure*, how *embarrassing*!"

Clearly I am from the school of, "A penny saved is a penny earned." She, on the other hand, is from the school of, "Why would anyone pick up a worthless nickel?"

At the end of the day there was so much change on the floor you could easily pick up as much as fifty cents just walking to the office.

Pens and pencils are, at least in the minds of kids, disposable, too. At the end of the day the floor is littered with them. Never mind that half the freshmen class never has a pen or pencil when they need them. Dozens and dozens of them still end up on the floor.

And textbooks? Well, as far as many kids are concerned, these five-pound, $60 books are disposable, too. Once when following behind a bus from my school, I actually saw one get tossed out the window.

And even more astounding than that, at the end of the year, when kids are offered the opportunity to go through the huge pile of unclaimed books on the chance that theirs was turned in by someone else, they won't do it. Most won't take the time to look through the pile for their book, but would rather let their parents pay the $60 to replace it. It would have taken them, perhaps, half an hour to go through the pile. Would you work for $120 an hour?

The lost and found in a high school is amazing, too. You could clothe a small village with what is sitting in the lost and found. Dozens of pairs of eyeglasses. Expensive coats. Jewelry. Cameras. Hundred dollar tennis shoes. Full book bags. Notebooks. Even photo albums. Once after a dance a suit coat was left, and was never picked up.

Pennies, pencils, and textbooks may seem trivial, but the lessons must start somewhere.

Don't buy into our society's notion that if a kid doesn't have everything that every other kid has, he's going to be scarred for life. Stuff breaks and goes out of style.

But the lessons about the value of that stuff, those will last a lifetime.

There's a Lifetime Lost in the Black Hole of the Backpack

He jumped up next to his desk when the bell rang—all eighty-eight knock-kneed pounds of him. He hefted the brand new backpack filled with twenty-five pounds of just-issued textbooks, slung it over his shoulder—and the laws of physics kicked in. Weight and momentum carried the pack to the other side of his seat and, like a slow motion cartoon, pulled that poor, astonished freshman to the ground nose first, feet in the air. The backpack landed on the floor with a thud, with him still attached to it.

That story is true. I swear I didn't crack a smile. I swear. But I almost burst from keeping it inside.

Ah, yes, the backpack: hider of secrets, desktop pillow, personal billboard, and weapon of class destruction, its disorganized contents being a contributing factor to failure.

High school—especially big high schools—can be an unsettling adjustment after the relative comfort of junior high. Lockers can be far from classes and passing time is short—too short if you ask the kids, who live for those five minutes of bliss, hanging with friends and sneaking cell phone calls. But it's plenty long if you ask the principals who watch the kids hang with friends and sneak cell phone calls—then rush late to class.

Thus, into the backpack everything goes so no time is wasted stopping at a locker. Parents who brave a peek into backpacks might be surprised by what they find. In addition to the textbooks, iPod, liter of pop, heap of candy wrappers, Game Boy, and the odd smelly gym shirt, there's a wad of paper hard and heavy enough to use as a doorstop, as assignments and handouts get shoved in on top of each other, never making it into the folders that you bought at the beginning of the year. Over time those papers mold together into expressionistic, abstract sculpturesque works of art.

Hour after hour, day after day, week after week, papers are shoved in and promptly forgotten. That assignment you saw him work on last night that never got turned in? Still in the backpack. The permission slip he said he lost? Still in the backpack. Instructions for the big marking period project in history? Still in the backpack. The interim report you never saw? Yep, sucked into the black hole of the backpack.

Trust me on this. I taught freshmen for fifteen years. Lack of organization contributes to their failure as much as anything else.

And while the backpack seems to hold the very lifeblood of the student, kids can be surprisingly blasé about them, too. Just check your school's lost and found and see how many bulging backpacks sit abandoned, never to be claimed by fickle owners who simply purchase a new one and move on.

Oh, and my falling freshman? Well, by the end of the year he had grown into his backpack.

All that weight lifting, I suppose.

Diligence Gets Kids through Freshman Year

"I just don't understand. She's always done so well in school," said the puzzled parents of freshmen, hundreds of times in my teaching career.

They're referring to what I call the Freshman Phenomenon: students who had been reasonably successful K–8 suddenly, inexplicably, start doing poorly in school.

Ask any teacher and they will tell you that most students do not do poorly in school because they can't do the work. They do poorly in school because they won't do the work.

So my theory, based on fifteen years of teaching predominantly freshman journalism classes, is that this low performance has more to do with growing pains than academics.

Once when I had a particularly difficult year teaching eighth grade, a principal told me that the early adolescent years were all about social and emotional growth, with very little brain growth. That was comforting, because it seemed that those eighth graders had three speeds: uncontrollable giggling, yelling, or crying.

And since freshmen were just eighth graders, it's not surprising that they're still growing emotionally and socially.

At the root of the problem is a preoccupation with looks, popularity, social status, fitting in, and tantalizing distractions provided by older, streetwise kids. Freshmen girls, for example, fuss endlessly with their hair and makeup. By the time they're seniors, they stop. If you were to hear a tape of what goes through a freshman's mind, I'm sure 98 percent of it would involve one insecurity after another. Preoccupation equals forgetfulness. "But I *saw* you do that assignment!" parents would exclaim. "Why didn't you turn it in?!" "I just forgot," the child would reply.

Kids go from the relative safety of junior high, replete with warm fuzzies, to the fast, sometimes impersonal, pace of high school. If getting around a large building isn't challenging enough, now their classes count for credit.

The work is more difficult and demanding and there's a lot less handholding. A late assignment is marked down, and missed assignments pile up fast. It's easy to fall so far behind that students are overwhelmed.

Work ethic is at issue, too. If students haven't been taught responsibility at home, they don't have the skills to buckle down when the going gets tough.

Another huge problem for freshmen is organization. Look into a freshman's book bag and you're likely to find a lot of "lost" papers. I don't know which comes first, the disorganized book bag or the disorganized mind, but I do know that it equals lost handouts and lost homework. For many freshmen, simply remembering to bring a textbook to class is a colossal feat.

The heartening news is that in most cases, my freshmen pulled their acts together by sophomore year. That's not good enough, though, because failed freshman classes put them behind in credits, compromising graduation.

We don't need new legislation or a different curriculum to save our freshmen. But we do need all hands on deck to guide them through these turbulent years.

The Parking Lot Belongs to the Students

When I was learning to drive, my mom told me to be especially careful when driving past a bar. People were apt to pull out without looking, she said.

I'd like to offer the same advice to people driving past high schools on warm afternoons in the spring. Because nowhere is spring celebrated more exuberantly than in a high school parking lot.

The first brush of warm air has kids bursting from the building with the bell, young men stripping off shirts, warm sun on skinny, winter white chests. Out come the cell phones (who are they calling?) and on go the caps. Some carry backpacks, but many don't (no homework?), arms swinging loose and free.

A strut to the car, enjoying the walk, hoots and hollers, heys and high fives. Cars still parked haphazardly from the morning rush to first hour, kids creating parking spots where there are none.

"Come on, I'll give you a ride!" kids yell to anyone and everyone, any excuse just to stay in this car a little longer, windows down, eardrums aching with the thumping, jumping, bumping music that defines them. To see and be seen through the anonymity of sunglasses, letting the choice of music tell their story.

The cars are much nicer now than they were when I was in high school, and more kids have them, but there's still variety, from the beater to the sublime. Kids' lives revolve around long hours at menial jobs to pay for those wheels.

As June draws close the high jinks get wilder, and sunning on the roofs of cars turns to dancing on the roofs of cars.

More expansive in the parking lot than they would ever be inside the school, the unlikeliest of kids talk to each other. In the safety and familiarity of their cars they casually light up, looking authority in the eye, daring us to bust them.

It's the meeting place, the show-off place, and on weekends occasionally the party place, judging by the brown bottles rolling through on Monday morning.

With school personnel at a premium it's usually the least patrolled place too, resulting in too much theft, vandalism, and the dealing of drugs.

When they finally leave, it's jackrabbit starts and the irresistible tire squeal—"Look at me! Look at me!" fast and careless, heady with horsepower.

The down side of all this exuberance is the regularity of fender benders, in the parking lot and in front of the school; inexperienced drivers dazed by the hot sun and their own coolness.

And though the morning parking lot is busy too, the mood is frantic, not buoyant. In the morning the mad dash is sleepy kids racing to beat the bell.

So if bad timing puts you in front of a high school at dismissal, roll down your windows, crank up your radio, put on your sunglasses, and recapture your youth.

Just make sure you drive defensively.

The Shuffled Children

I call them the Shuffled Children.

Every teacher knows them. Actually, teachers know a lot of them. And for every shuffled child they know of in their classes, there are a dozen that they don't know about.

I'll bet you know some Shuffled Children, too. They're the kids who are shuffled back and forth between their estranged parents' houses several times a week.

Sometimes these kids know the shuffle-schedule. Other times they don't know for sure where they will be on any given night.

The Shuffled Children may not have a time or place where they can get their homework done. Often they spend evenings with a parent running errands or visiting relatives. They might try to study for a test in the car. Quite often they come to school without their backpacks or other materials, having left them at one parent's house, or the other.

Sometimes they can't get the backpack until the next time they see that parent. Their teachers will be frustrated if they don't have their schoolwork with them. But not having their schoolwork is the least of these kids' worries.

Teachers are never sure which parent to call when there's a problem. And they get conflicting stories when they finally do reach a parent. Sometimes one parent expresses frustration, even anger, with the other parent's parenting. This makes the teacher uncomfortable. It makes the child even more uncomfortable.

The Shuffled Children might have two bedrooms, one at each parent's house. The rules at each might be different. This is confusing to the child. But they'll take advantage of it if they can.

There are other kinds of Shuffled Children, too. Like the ones who are shuffled from one living situation to another. You know the story: Mom moves in with her boyfriend, or Dad moves in with his girlfriend, and the child has to move, too. It doesn't work out, so they move again. Eventually she meets a new guy, he meets a new girl, and they believe once again that this is The One. But it's not. So they'll move. Again.

Sometimes the new boyfriend or girlfriend has kids, too. Suddenly, there are two sets of kids sharing bedrooms, bathrooms, and most important, their parent, with virtual strangers day in, day out. Often these households don't have any kind of a schedule or routine. Basically, it's every kid for herself. There aren't many Brady Bunch moments. The kids may or may not like Mom's or Dad's new friend. After all, they don't really even know them, do they?

No one asks the kids how they feel about all this. No one prepares them for it. This huge lifestyle change makes them sad and scared and angry. It's hard to concentrate at school when you're worried about where you'll sleep tonight. Eventually, out of anger and frustration, they act up in class.

This moving from living situation to living situation often involves a change of school district. So not only is the child shuffled, but transcripts are shuffled, too. In some urban schools, at the end of the school year the teachers have almost none of the same kids they started the school year with.

Sometimes the child moves into and out of the same school district several times. Teachers and office workers do the paperwork for the check-out process, only to have to do it again when the child reenrolls a few months later.

Sometimes moving makes these kids miss important material that's covered in class. Sometimes they get the same material twice. But once again, schoolwork is the least of their worries.

After all, they have to make new friends, learn new routines, find their way around new buildings, bus routes, and classes. Their new teachers have new rules and different ways of doing things. That's a lot of scary new stuff to learn. Who has time to worry about schoolwork?

Unless they happen to be unusually resilient, the world doesn't feel like a safe place to the Shuffled Children. How could it when their home life can change on a whim?

The Shuffled Children.

It's not their fault.

I Had the Strangest Dream

Maybe it was the four tacos with hot sauce I ate before going to bed last night, but I had the strangest dream . . .

Out they came, swaggering, strutting, heads held high. They were the best and they knew it. This victory against their rival team had been hard won. They'd fought and scrabbled for every point. Privately they'd worried a bit that they wouldn't be able to pull it off, but Coach had assured them they were ready, and Coach was always right.

Hours, days, weeks of practice had finally paid off, and the state semi-final contest was over. Now they were headed for the championships, hoping, wishing, and fervently dreaming of that state title. Still wearing team colors, they filed out into the hall where cheering fans and the press waited. They stepped into the throng.

"You handled the pressure very well. How did you prepare?" asked a reporter.

"Well, we've got Coach Fisher to thank for that. He took us through every conceivable scenario, so we were ready for anything," answered Robbie, the team captain.

"Robbie, Robbie, over here! WJRT-TV! Can you tell us what was going through your mind in the final minutes?"

"I just knew if we could pick up those last points it would seal the victory for us," he said.

Reporters crowded around, a mass of bright lights and microphones. Fans, too, were trying to get the attention of one team member or another. Everyone wanted to be close to the team, to be able to say they were there, and they knew them when.

When they got to school the next day, balloons and posters signed in glitter pen by friends, covered their lockers. All day congratulations and high fives came from kids they didn't even know. Even teachers paused in their lesson plans to comment on the victory.

"Hey, way to go last night!"

"You were smokin'!"

"I can't believe it, they didn't stand a chance!"

"You guys made them look like *babies!*"

Tickets to the championship were as valuable and hard to come by as a Jimmy Buffett concert. Principal O'Brian finally announced that they would be sold by lottery. Everyone grumbled, but the principal maintained that it was the only fair way. Lines for the lottery wound all the way down the hall.

On game day, kids eagerly crowded into the gym, to the special assembly being held in the team's honor. Stomping, screaming, they cheered themselves hoarse, feeling as if the team's victory was their victory, impressed and awed by their heroes.

Heads filled with game strategy, the team was nevertheless able to enjoy the moment, rise to the occasion.

The student frenzy. The community enthusiasm. The statewide attention. The pride. The recognition. The prestige. The scholarship buzz.

All this, because the state title was within reach for the Quiz Bowl Team.

Huh? . . . Wait a minute—*what*?!

Mental prowess prized as much as physical prowess?!

It must have been the tacos.

Average Children, Lost in the Crowd

She sits somewhere in the middle of the classroom.

She's quiet. She's polite. She doesn't contribute to class discussions. She doesn't have many friends and she doesn't get in trouble. She does her schoolwork most of the time, on time. It is not awful, or outstanding.

She doesn't participate in extracurricular activities. She comes to school and goes home, never staying for a meeting or a practice.

Her looks are average. Not homely. Not beautiful. Nothing much distinguishes her from anyone else.

This is the average child. The middle child. And because she neither excels nor fails she gets less attention than the spectacular, or the spectacularly bad, child.

Reams of legislation are passed, and billions of dollars are spent, to protect and nurture the academically challenged children. And precocious, talented, high achieving children naturally command their share of the spotlight. But in the classroom, just like in many families, the middle children never seem to get their due.

I once overheard a colleague make a deal with a truant student to improve his attendance. "If you come to school for two weeks straight I'll take you out for pizza," she said. One of the average children heard, too. "I come to school every day," she said. "What do I get?"

Often, the middle children prefer their anonymity, especially the painfully shy ones. Their eyes plead with you to let them hide quietly behind their books. It seems most kind to let them.

My first year in the classroom, a wise, experienced teacher cautioned me to make sure to spend a few moments with those quiet children each day, to make a point of offering a comment or praise. If you don't, she said, they might fall through the cracks.

It hurts to admit it, but like a busy parent trying to juggle too much, I didn't always get around to having that quiet moment with the middle children. Twenty-eight students in fifty-five minutes meant less than two minutes each—if I had nothing to do but talk to kids. But of course, that wasn't the case. There was that five-pound textbook to get through, and all of that documentation to complete. Backtalkers, spitball throwers, cell phone sneakers, homework deadbeats, bad attitudes, class clowns—and yes, the perfectionist high achievers, too, all take time and attention away from the average child.

I feel bad about every middle child that did not get enough of my attention. If there is one single thing I would have done differently, it would be to close the textbook, set aside the lesson plan, stop rushing, and sit right down with that quiet child.

"What are you thinking about?" I would ask.

And I would listen hard for the answer.

Seniors Take Heed

Trust me, it's most unbecoming to beg.

So seniors, heed this: if you let the senioritis bug bite you, you may spend your last days of school begging.

Begging your teachers to pass you, that is.

It happened every year that I taught, and it was a pitiful sight to see every time. At least one student would completely blow off the last marking period of his senior year, ignore all warnings from teachers, fail a class, lose a credit, and end up not graduating. So that last day of school, which should have been filled with nostalgia and celebration, instead became a sorrowful experience as he begged his teacher to please, please, please, pass him so he could walk on graduation day.

Sometimes it worked. Sometimes it didn't. Either way, it was wrenching for all involved. And whatever you may think of your teachers, when you fail it's as painful for them as it is for you.

So seniors take heed. Once you return from spring break (and whatever temptations you faced there) the temptation to let it all go and revel in your senior status will be as alluring as the smell of a flame-broiled Whopper.

True, the sprint to the finish line is stressful. Significant life decisions about college or jobs can fill even the most levelheaded student with self-doubt. My guess is that stress is one reason seniors give in—it's easier to decree that senioritis has claimed mind and body than to make the hard decisions.

Ironically, right when students need to be in top form to pull it all together, they are hit with a lassitude that, real or not, can be contagious. "I have senioritis!" becomes synonymous with "I don't want to do any work today," and can start a dangerous chain reaction. To teens it's an accepted rite of passage, one that feels wickedly fun, to boot.

Demands for end-of-year projects at school compete with distractions at home where there's often a frenzy of home improvement projects in preparation for the graduation open house. And it's expensive to be a senior. Senior pictures, graduation announcements, new clothes, prom, and open houses all take their toll on the family budget.

So to parents I say, this is not the time to relax your own vigilance. Do not take the role of enabler and ease up on the rules. Consistency is key. Don't be afraid to be the heavy.

Of course, academics are not the only way a senior year can go awry. A prank that seems harmless can have devastating disciplinary consequences, too.

So seniors please, don't make your teachers deliver that one final lesson—that you are accountable for the work and will fail if you don't do it.

Finish what you started. You can choose for this to be a joyful, productive time, or you can choose to disappoint your parents, and ultimately, yourself.

Choose wisely.

The Most Wonderful Day of the Year

"Na na na na, Na na na na, Hey hey hey, Goodbye. Na na na na, Na na na na, Hey, seniors, Goodbye."

I stood in the doorway of my classroom watching the senior class walk arm in arm down the hall, singing. I clenched my teeth to keep from blubbering, but when I looked over at the teacher in the next doorway, she was wiping her eyes.

And why shouldn't we cry like sentimental fools? After all, this is what it's all about for us, the reward of our life's work. Thirteen years of education culminate in this celebration. We're proud, happy, gratified.

And wary. After all, anything can happen on this, the seniors' last day of school. Pumped, manic, intoxicated with nostalgia, the students fairly throb with emotion. We've threatened them with everything we can think of, including not walking down the aisle at graduation, to keep them from doing something stupid today.

It started at 5:30 a.m., when seniors, most of whom were hard-pressed all year to drag themselves out of bed and get here on time, arrived in the school parking lot. They made banners and signs, painted their faces and clothes, and entered the building singing, just before the first bell.

Security was here early, too, and principals and hall monitors and teachers. Not interfering. Just watching. Just in case.

Because until that last bell rings at 2:15, it's all about containment, at least for staff. Undergrads bounce off the walls, too, caught up in the excitement. Little real teaching will happen today.

Some teachers give tests in an effort to keep students focused. Others have parties, adding to the hysteria by way of sugar-high. Missed deadlines caused by acute senioritis require many kids to spend the day completing projects, slap-dashing them together, racing to turn them in.

It's an all-day hug-fest, kids suddenly clinging to people they've never even talked to. Camcorders record every last smile, cameras flash endlessly, memory books are passed around and signed.

Some students, unfortunately, spend the day cajoling, bribing, and flat-out begging teachers to pass them, in spite of having had multiple warnings of impending failure. It's heartbreaking for teachers to have to deliver this one last lesson: you must do the work in order to earn the grade. Tears over leaving good friends mingle with tears over poor grades and failure.

It's a thrilling, demanding, exhausting day, and when that last bell rings, we roll our eyes heavenward and say a little prayer of thanks. The whoops and hollers crescendo as kids pour out of the building. When the last car squeals out of the parking lot, we at last breathe easily. The sudden hush is blissful.

We've done our part. The seniors are finally gone, and we're glad to see them go. But it's relief mixed with apprehension. After all, for seniors, the celebrating has just begun.

No longer under our protective wing, they're off doing God knows what, God knows where.

CHAPTER 5

Student Issues

BOYS AND GIRLS, BIRDS AND BEES, THE NATURE OF THE BEAST

Put Some Clothes On, Girl

You shouldn't stare, but face it, it's hard not to. High school girls are pushing dress code limits like never before.

The warm months are the true test of a high school's dress code, namely in the form of itsy-bitsy teeny-weeny clothes that not-so-itsy-bitsy teeny-weeny girls wear.

Educators don't want to deal with dress codes. We have better things to do. But if you're going to let them out of the house like that, then we're going to have to bust them when they get here.

It's not about morality. Parents have made it more than clear that they don't want public schools to teach values.

For school personnel it's about disruption. It takes no more than a change in the wind to distract a teenager from the task at hand, especially if they aren't all that keen on the task to begin with. And the lure of a tush peeking out from under microshorts, breasts being pushed up out of shirts, and thongs riding up out of low rider jeans is a big-time distraction.

I believe that students need the freedom to express themselves. I also happen to think that many of the latest styles for girls are cute. But school isn't a party, and anything that distracts from the work at hand is a problem, just as it would be in the workplace.

One day one of my former colleagues stepped up to the podium at the beginning of his second period history class, only to look down at the front row and see a sophomore girl wearing an extremely low-cut top. More of her chest showed than didn't, and on her breast was a great big purple hickey.

Did you gasp?

If you haven't spent time in a high school recently you may have.

If she's brazen enough to come to school like that, then she's wearing that hickey like a medal of honor and she's not going to take kindly to being disciplined for showing it.

You know the kids have seen it. You know they're talking about it, or at the very least thinking about it. How interesting is the Civil War going to be when the hottie next to you has a hickey on her breast?

Then she'll say that she wore this shirt to school before and no one said anything. And that may or may not be true. Sometimes teachers get so busy that they just don't notice what every kid in every class is wearing. Sometimes they choose not to notice. Why add more aggravation to an already aggravating day?

Referring her to the office will likely result in a showdown. She'll want to know just what, exactly, is wrong with her outfit, making the teacher explain out loud what is inappropriate. The rest of the class will likely back her up.

Mentioning the shirt is suicide enough—but the hickey? Don't even go there. It's a no-win conversation. "It's not a hickey, it's a birthmark, and what are you doing looking there anyway (you creepy old pervert)?" she'll say.

And there you have it. One girl's inappropriate attire has just wasted ten minutes of this teacher's time and the time of every student in that class. Imagine countless variations of that story and you know what high schools are dealing with in the warm months. Multiply that by hundreds of kids, and—you get the picture.

True story: another colleague had a girl strut into his class and defiantly flop into her chair wearing a T-shirt that read, in large capital letters, "GODDESS OF FUCK!"

He just shook his head.

And handed her a pass to the office.

The X-Rated Boogie

Chaperoning the prom used to be fun. The glitz, glamour, elegance, and excess of a senior prom are truly something to see. But the excess is no longer reserved for expensive gowns and huge limousines. Now, not only is the attire excessive, but the behavior is, too.

Chaperoning used to be easy. You really only had to watch for the basic stuff: smoking, a fight brewing, or maybe a couple making out in a dark corner. And because kids' behavior really does improve when they're dressed like grown-ups, problems were few and far between. But in recent years, chaperoning any event that involves teenagers and music has become a battle of wills as teens pump, thump, bump, and hump to the music of their generation.

We call it dirty dancing.

They call it a generation gap.

The last few proms I chaperoned were spent patrolling the dance floor, continuously telling kids to either clean it up, or leave. One incident was so outrageous it left me shaken.

I approached this particular group because about two dozen kids had formed a tight circle, all facing inward, clapping and cheering at whatever was going on in the middle.

When I finally pushed through the crowd, it took me a minute to process what I saw. My first impression was of a beautiful girl wearing a long white gown, made of some slinky jersey material. Backless and low-cut in front, it was just a slip of a dress, but it looked absolutely gorgeous on her long lanky frame.

But—what? What was this?! She was bent over at the waist, hands planted firmly on her thighs, pumping her rear up and down in time to the music. Her long blond hair hung down around her shoulders, obscuring her face from view. Against her backside, with his pelvis pressed tightly against her rear, was a young man in a tuxedo. He was holding her firmly by the shoulders as he, too, pumped to the music.

Was she . . . being held there against her will?! I rushed over.

"Let go of her this instant!" I growled.

The boy laughed. And kept pumping. The crowd of kids kept clapping.

"Go, go, go!" they chanted.

I looked around, confused. What were they cheering for?

Suddenly I got it. Like spectators at a sporting event, they were egging the couple on.

I moved in closer. The girl still had her head down, hair swinging from side to side.

"Stop!" I commanded. The boy laughed and spun off. The girl stood up, flipped her hair back, and laughed.

"*What?*" she asked, exasperated.

"Are you okay?" I asked.

"Uh, *yeah*," she said sarcastically.

"What were you thinking then, letting that boy do that to you?" I asked.

"We were *dancing*," she said.

"That was *not* dancing," I replied. "Would you dance like that in front of your mother?"

"My mother taught me," she said snottily, again with the hair flip.

I know that her mother didn't teach her that. I doubt her mother had any idea that she danced like that. In fact, I'll bet most of you don't know how your kids dance. Because if you're watching, they're probably giving you the PG version of an X-rated boogie.

Since that prom I have had countless conversations with kids about the way they dance. And I have been told, over and over and over again, that I, like most adults, am hopelessly old-fashioned, that I just don't get it, it doesn't mean a thing, it's just the way they dance.

To combat the issue, many schools have created guidelines for dances, stating that any action that simulates sex is taboo. Some have forbidden the DJ to play certain songs. Some have gone so far as to make kids sign a contract when they purchase their tickets, agreeing that they won't dance dirty.

Perhaps the only real solution is for parents to get involved and attend dances. If they do, though, I recommend they have the paramedics standing by, because those parents are going to be left breathless, speechless, and blinded by what they see.

Kids on the Cutting Edge

I glanced down as I handed Chris his English assignment. What I saw made me gasp out loud. Raw, bloody, screaming red, scabby streaks ran down the entire length of his arm. For almost a minute I did nothing but stare dumbly, trying to process what I saw. I looked up at his face, then back down at his arm.

"My God, Chris, what happened to your arm?!" I asked. He jerked it back quickly and pulled down his sleeve. I gathered my wits and asked him to go into the hall with me, then asked him to show me his arm again. He did so, reluctantly. I looked more closely. The scabs seemed to form letters: M-A-N-S-O-N.

I was shocked. And repulsed. And sort of angry, the way you are when someone does something stupid to get attention.

"You did this to yourself," I said. The cuts were too perfect to have been an accident. He didn't answer.

"Why?" I asked.

He wouldn't look up, just squirmed, uncomfortable, head down. "It's nothing. Just something I do for fun," he said.

"Fun?" I asked. "*Fun*?! Didn't it *hurt*?" I tried to imagine taking a sharp object to my own flesh, purposely breaking the skin and then going over and over the same spot, watching it bleed, and still not stopping.

"No," he said.

Many times in my teaching career I felt at a loss, but never more than that day. I was way out of my league and I knew it. I sent Chris off to see his counselor.

At that time, I knew nothing about self-injury, or "cutting." To those of us who whine about a paper cut, understanding the mind-set of a cutter is difficult. According to cutters, cutting themselves provides rapid, if temporary, relief of anxiety, anger, and agitation. They say that it's a release valve, a way of getting back to reality when they feel disassociated from themselves. They say the physical pain lessens the emotional pain.

After researching self-injury, I thought about Chris. Was he angry? He was a nice kid, never caused a problem in class. And yet, I did feel his anger sometimes, simmering just below the surface.

Most cutters do not carve designs into their skin like Chris did. Most just cut, usually their wrists, arms, thighs, or stomach, using anything they have handy: a disposable razor, broken glass, even plastic silverware.

There is no particular "type" of kid who cuts, though it is more often girls than boys, and usually starts in early adolescence. A feeling of invalidation seems to be the most common characteristic, the sense that they are not allowed to have, or show, their true feelings. They have a sense of powerlessness, and cutting makes them feel in control.

Sometimes self-injury is contagious, and the habit spreads and is mimicked by others. It turns into almost a fad at some schools, as it did in the late 1980s at my school. Female students went through a phase where they carved the names of their boyfriends into their arms, using pins, or the sharp point of the wire from a spiral notebook.

I didn't see any more evidence of Chris's cutting that year, but that doesn't mean he wasn't doing it. Cutters are sneaky. Because of the social stigma attached, they hide their wounds, literally and figuratively. Contrary to what I thought when I first saw Chris's arm, they don't do it for attention. They don't do it to annoy others. It has little to do with anyone but them.

Other forms of self-injury include burning, self-hitting, interference with wound healing, hair pulling, and bone breaking, though cutting is the most common.

There are few statistics available, but experts estimate that 4 percent of adolescents in the United States purposely hurt themselves in some way. And they believe that the number is rising.

It's a dangerous, complicated illness. Asking or ordering a self-injurer to stop rarely works. If you need help, call 1-800-DONTCUT, or go to www.siari.co.uk or www.selfinjury.com.

Homework Means Work at Home

If you listen to the hype about homework, you're probably as confused as I am. Too much? Too little? It depends on which study you read.

Of course, kids don't like homework. But more and more, parents feel like it's an imposition, too. I always came away from parent–teacher conferences shaking my head. Was I giving too much homework? Or not enough? The answer depended on which parent you asked.

After twenty years in the classroom I do have two strong impressions about the homework dilemma. The first is that many kids seem to feel that we have no right to give them homework. In some convoluted reasoning, being protected from homework is, to them, similar to being protected from corporal punishment or verbal abuse.

The attitude of some kids is that homework is a violation of their rights. There's sort of a "You can make me do schoolwork while I'm here, but your rights don't extend into my home life" attitude.

Our litigious society has taught them to look for every loophole, too. I had the following conversation with a freshman that missed school and wanted class time to make up her work. (In fact, I had variations of this conversation with students almost daily . . . you can see why teachers sometimes feel like banging their heads against the wall.)

Student: (*worried, panicked voice*) "Ms. Flynn, it's not fair, I wasn't here yesterday, do I get extra time to work on this newspaper project?"

Me: (*calm, neutral voice*) "Yes, you may take it home and finish it and turn it in the day after tomorrow."

Student: "Well, I don't get the newspaper at home, so I can't."

Me: "I have lots of newspapers. Take as many as you need."

Student: "But it's not my fault I was absent. I was sick."

Me: "Well, whatever the reason, you still have to make up the work if you want a grade. And you can't do it in class because you'll miss what we're doing today and get further behind."

Student: "Well, I don't have *time* to do it at home!"

Me: (*shrugging*) "Well, that's how it works. When you're absent you have to do your make-up work at home."

Student: (*stomping off angrily*) "*It's not my fault I got the flu!*"

Parents don't want to hear the second thing that I found to be true about homework.

Kids lie.

Parents repeatedly told me that their child came home every night and said they didn't have homework. When I showed them the grade book and all of the homework assignments that their child had not done, their response was plaintive: "Well, there's nothing I can do if he lies to me about it!"

Once during a discussion with my class about study habits, I asked my students if their parents ever inquired about their homework. I'll never forget what one freshman said. He candidly told me that whenever his mom asked if he had his homework done, he purposely mumbled. He would turn the other way and leave the room, and mumble over his shoulder. He said it worked every time and she always let it go. He said he didn't feel bad about it because he wasn't actually lying. (Poor kid. It didn't occur to him that I'd tell his mom what he said.)

Oh, and that old excuse about the dog eating their homework?

It's been replaced.

The printer ate it.

Still No Girls Allowed
in Good Old Boys Club

Mothers, take heed: the good old boys club is alive and well in your daughter's school, and she's still being left out of it.

I spent fourteen years advising student publications and worked closely with the same group of students, mostly girls, for four years at a stretch, in a team-like setting.

I come from a family of girls, so imagine my surprise the first time I had a staff with a lot of boys. Locker-room jokes and roughhousing aside, the good old boys instinct was as natural to them as breathing.

I watched, amazed. The least talented of the group were treated by the other boys as if they were stars, and the most talented as if they were gods. Backslapping and high-fiving, they sang each others' praises endlessly. One of them might be an absolute twit, but if he was part of the club, he was golden. And the twits, thanks to their buddies, will probably be pulling six-figure salaries someday.

If I came down on one of them for something, the rest of the group jumped to his defense, sighing, eye-rolling, and arguing. As a mere female my opinion was as insignificant to them as the rest of the girls.'

Private jokes and insider stories prevailed, to the exclusion of everyone else. Forget about staff teamwork. They were their own team.

Don't get me wrong. I liked these boys. They were funny and smart and basically, kind. But I got an up-close-and-personal look at how the good old boys club works. I just didn't know how early it starts.

I also didn't know how completely left out of it girls were. Girls, who were twice as talented as those boys, were often cowed by them.

For better or worse, the girls just didn't have that camaraderie, that unity. Rarely did they compliment each other or stick up for each other. They didn't stick up for themselves, either.

The women's movement seems to have bypassed our girls in a number of ways. Things that were de rigueur to me growing up in the 1970s are a mystery to girls today.

For example, I decided early on that I would keep my maiden name when I married. It wasn't a political statement. Just a very strong sense of self.

I also don't wear a wedding ring, though I am, happily, married. These two topics served to absolutely confound my female students year after year. Every time a new group of students figured out that my husband was the history teacher down the hall with the different last name, they would scratch their heads in wonder.

"But why don't you want people to know you're married?" the girls would ask. "Is it a secret?" Or, "What's with this 'Ms.' thing?" Inevitably this was followed with, "When I get married I *want* to take my husband's last name . . . and he'd *better* buy me a really big ring!"

My explanations about being your own person while sharing your life with another fell on deaf ears. They just didn't get it.

Somehow, we're missing the target with our girls. Girl Power seems to be more about the right to dress slutty than about true empowerment. Teen magazines encourage girls to "be themselves," but only in reference to the clothes they wear or the hairstyles they choose.

Granted, the women's movement and Title IX have ensured that girls will be allowed to take woodshop (at my high school in 1972 I couldn't) and have the same sports teams the boys have. But thirty-some years later I just don't see the kind of fundamental change in girls that I would hope for.

How would empowerment look on a teenage girl? Decisive. Assertive. Independent. Supportive of other girls.

Moms, talk to your girls. Just saying, "You can be anything you want to be when you grow up," is not enough.

Tell them that they are strong. Tell them that when they boost other girls they don't detract from themselves. Tell them that they don't need to look for their self-worth in the eyes of a boy.

Tell them to form their own damn club.

Searching for a Female Role Model

Quick, list three positive role models for young girls.

Okay, now try it again, only this time, don't include any athletes.

Pretty tough, huh?

Now list three not-so-positive role models for girls. Bet that was much easier, wasn't it?

It seems that everywhere I look I see examples of how I don't want young girls to be. Exceptions abound in the world of sports with strong role models in the WNBA, college athletics, and the Olympics. But what about girls who don't play sports?

I pondered this in light of the passing of Betty Friedan, author of *The Feminine Mystique*. Though I didn't read it until college, as a high school girl I heard my mom talk about its premise that women could have interests other than husbands and families, and should aspire to separate identities.

Forty years later, it's a message that girls still need to hear.

What astounds me about my female students is how oblivious they are of the women's movement. They still think that the boy is the prize, a concept that's reinforced by silly young women fighting over one man on reality television shows like *The Bachelor*. Fistfights between girls at school are almost always over a boy. And way too many girls are still willing to change their friends, their look, their personality, and their interests for a boy.

I listened when my mom talked about Betty Friedan and Gloria Steinem, but it was Marcia Brady I aspired to be. A watered-down feminist to be sure, but at least she was wholesome. Unfortunately, many examples of young womanhood today are not.

And that's the rub, isn't it? The ones we would choose to be our daughters' role models are not necessarily who they would choose for themselves.

Still, we have to try. If our girls prefer the half-dressed writhers on music videos, or slutty looking little dolls called Bratz, or vapid pop stars, we need to counter that with examples of substance. Jessica Simpson may be a business tycoon, but that's not why girls emulate her.

Part of the problem is that we only give girls half the message. "You can be anything you want" we tell them, and leave it at that. We need to have the entire conversation, including some good strong examples of what they could be. We need to show them how to get there. We need to, somehow, make them hear the message that, yes, boys are nice, but they're the icing, not the cake.

Girls who believe that the boy is the prize, lose the real prize: themselves. I want girls to quit looking to boys for validation. I want girls to put their own interests ahead of a boy's.

I want to hear girls tell boys, unequivocally, "I've got things to do. But you're welcome to come along for the ride."

Homecoming Queen: as Outdated as English Monarchy

She's pretty, she's sweet, and although she doesn't know it, she's also hopelessly out of style. I'm talking about the homecoming queen.

High schools, ironically, institutions that strive for political correctness, continue to support a contest that objectifies girls almost as much as most music videos.

Years ago, when the idea of homecoming queen was conceived women had very different roles. Their worth was judged on their looks and the mate they won. Once married, they were judged on their cooking and the cleanliness of the house they kept.

But it's the twenty-first century and we're still clinging to this obsolete measure of a girl. It's way past time that our daughters aspire to something more than a popularity contest.

I want girls to have a sense of accomplishment that comes from within, rather than from without. I want girls to know that they're special and powerful because of what they can do, not how they look. And I don't want this silly contest to dim the confidence of girls who don't "make the cut."

We can choose to expose girls to experiences that empower them, where they are judged on what they can do, or we can continue to promote an archaic contest where their sense of self-worth is bestowed by their peers.

In a weak attempt at equality, some schools have adopted a king contest, completely missing the point. Adding a king doesn't change the fact that contests for homecoming queen are fluff and fiction. After all, what, exactly does the homecoming queen excel in? Usually, at fitting in.

Unfortunately, the damage isn't only done to the queen and her court. Every other girl who wishes she was on that court receives the wrong message too, as does every boy who votes.

The very fact that we spend so much time and money on the homecoming queen contest tells girls we think it's important. It gets its own spread in the yearbook, is covered by the media, and class is even disrupted for assemblies and voting, clearly sending the message that we'll pull out all the stops for the pretty, popular girls.

Let's raise girls who are comfortable in their own skin. Let's raise girls who want to be measured by what they can do, not by their popularity. Let's teach girls to recognize homecoming queen contests for the shallow aspirations they are.

My guess is that many schools would like to drop the homecoming queen contest, but no one wants to be first. It's hard to challenge a long-standing tradition, even when it's wrong. If one school district does it though, the rest will follow.

I'm not saying that these girls aren't talented. I'm saying that this contest is never about talent. And I'm not saying we should abolish homecoming. It's a week filled with fun activities that build school spirit.

But the tradition of homecoming queen is obsolete. I know it, and you know it. Our girls just don't know it.

And they won't unless we tell them.

Boys Gone Bad

At first it just seemed like ordinary jostling in the crowded school halls. Four boys, walking elbow to elbow in a tight row, came up close behind her, almost stepping on her heels.

Suddenly she felt a hand reach around and cup her breast. Another hand grabbed her bottom and squeezed, hard. She gasped in fright and embarrassment, but was so tightly packed in by the crowd that she couldn't move away.

Whirling around, she came face to face with the laughing jeers of the four boys. Their hands were now in their pockets.

"Don't touch me!" she hissed.

"What?" the boys asked, eyes wide in feigned innocence. "What are you talking about?"

A high school principal described that scene to me. It's a growing problem, he said, and one of the most frustrating and time-consuming things he deals with.

But it's not only a problem at his school. The parent of a middle school child described the same thing in a letter to the syndicated advice column "Annie's Mailbox." The letter-writer expressed outrage that administrators at her daughter's school didn't put a stop to it.

It's not that perplexed school administrators aren't trying to stop it. But these boys are sly. They know that by traveling in a pack they make it difficult for the girl to identify which of them actually touched her. They're savvy enough to know that, even if guilty, they have as many rights as the victim.

And then they simply deny it. They know that without a witness, administrators have to be very careful about unjustly accusing the wrong person. Because while the girls' parents fiercely protect their daughters, the boys' parents just as fiercely protect their sons. After all, no parent wants to believe that their son is grabbing girls' breasts in public.

So why aren't there witnesses? Well, in today's super-sized schools where the students greatly outnumber the adults, you'd be surprised at how easy it is for kids to find long stretches of unsupervised hallway. Just like at home, kids know where the adults are. And where they aren't.

So what are principals to do? First, they'll bring the boys into their office one at a time and question them. They might even bring in another principal or a liaison officer and play good cop, bad cop. They'll try to catch the boys off guard and find inconsistencies in their stories. They'll question other students about what they saw.

Several hours out of the principal's day may be consumed with one incident. If the boys stick to their stories, though, there's not much more a principal can do.

Gone are the days when a boy who got fresh would get a swift, hard slap across the face from a girl. Today, that same slap may cause a girl to be suspended from school, or worse, charged with assault.

Girls are encouraged to speak up, not to suffer in silence but to get help from an adult. And some do. But for every girl who speaks up, are there several more that are afraid to for fear of retribution from the boys? After all, if the boys think little enough of them to harass them this way in public, what would they do to a girl who squealed?

The crux of the matter is why do the boys think this is okay? Might it have something to do with the music they listen to and the video games they play, where girls are objectified and called bitches, sluts, and hos? Might it be because their role models are based on celebrity, not character?

It bothers me that we focus on the girls, telling them to be brave and point fingers and name names. That's a start, but it doesn't put the onus where it belongs.

Don't assume that your son knows better. If you haven't talked to him about the proper way to treat a girl, who has?

It's Not the Kids, It's the Culture

"Will you tutor my daughter after class?" he asked earnestly. "This grade is not acceptable."

The man asking the question was the father of one of my freshmen. Her grade was an A–.

Is the fact that they were of Asian descent pertinent to that story? I don't know. I do know that during my teaching career in a highly diverse public school district, the dozens of Asian students I had placed an unparalleled value on education. Though their parents were not American born, and though they held vastly different religious and cultural beliefs than their peers, they flourished in the school system that is supposedly failing so many others. The American teen culture raging around them was not a distraction, so focused were they on their education.

And for some reason, I can't shake that memory as I contemplate the trend of single sex public schools.

It just seems like the easy way out.

We're hoping that single sex schools will fix what is largely (though not entirely) a cultural problem—parents who take no part in their children's education and a culture that embraces highly permissive parenting. We condone such nonsense as boy/girl sleepovers. We allow television to babysit and imprint our children from birth. We buy our kids a culture of silly female pop stars that encourage dumb girl stereotypes, and foul-mouthed rappers that dehumanize women.

Boys and girls *do* learn differently. But there are auditory, visual, kinesthetic, and tactile learners, too, and good teachers use strategies to reach all of them—in coed classrooms.

Reams of research support single sex education. Just as much research rejects it. But I'll bet the biggest reason the existing single sex schools work is that the parents who choose that setting for their kids are educated and involved and already place a premium on education. Just like the parents of my Asian students—parents who do not allow the hard sell of commercialism to interfere with their children's education; parents who recognize that teaching self-discipline is not punishment.

So I'm torn. I'm all for anything that is truly beneficial to the public school system. And if school district administrators say this is a good move for their particular clientele, I'm inclined to believe them.

And yet, I can't help but think that legislators love this idea because it is bold, and seemingly innovative, yet costs them nothing.

Simply separating girls from boys is not going to improve our indulgent American teen culture. Perhaps such legislation is proof of that indulgence.

My Asian students adapted and excelled within the given system. In America, we rearrange the system to accommodate the students.

Silence the Name-Callers

Blow queen. Faggot. Cocksucker. Fudge packer. Butt pirate. Dick licker. Dyke. Lesbo.

Ugly words, aren't they? It's hard for me to write them, and no doubt hard for you to read them. Imagine, then, hearing those names and worse, hissed at you in the halls of your school every day.

That's the reality for thousands of nonheterosexual students in this country, as they struggle with their sexual identity in a mean, cold place called high school.

Remember high school? Worrying about fitting in, wearing the right clothes, having the right friends? Even if you were popular, I'll bet you were riddled with private insecurities. Imagine, then, being a nonheterosexual student and keeping silent about a secret that, if known, would not only make you an outcast, but would so threaten some people that they would beat you up, just for the sport of it.

And what if you couldn't talk to your parents about it? Where would you turn?

Well, some fortunate students have the option of turning to gay–straight alliances at their schools, student clubs where any student—straight or not—can go for information and support.

Gay–straight alliances do not "promote" homosexuality or "encourage" kids to be gay. They simply provide information and support for questioning students. I attended a gay–straight alliance meeting in my town, and I watched ordinary high school kids, speaking ordinary kid-speak, joke and laugh and fool around, procrastinating like kids everywhere.

Then they got down to business, planning their annual Day of Silence. They discussed the statement to be printed on their Day of Silence T-shirts and cards. Then they watched a Barbara Walters interview with Rosie O'Donnell's partner, Kelli Carpenter, and discussed their own parents' attitudes toward gays.

I asked the kids what they got out of membership in this club. They answered without hesitation: "It's a sanctuary." "It fosters understanding."

"We provide an example for the rest of the school." "We can help educate people." "We can learn."

And there you have it: education. Gay–straight alliances offer questioning students solid information from reliable sources. Without that, vulnerable students turn to unsavory characters in Internet chat rooms, and fall into negative gay stereotypes of promiscuity, drugs, and even suicide.

Being gay is not a choice. But education is. We can always choose to open our minds and learn. I have high hopes that these brave kids will teach us.

Every April, youth across the country wear T-shirts and pass out cards on the Day of Silence in an effort to educate students and support safe schools and equality for all people, regardless of sexual orientation and gender identity or expression. Their hope is that this positive, collective, and audible silence will be the first step toward fighting harassment and prejudice.

And that, eventually, the name-callers will be silenced forever.

The Cola Wars: Cash for the Classroom

How does Pepsi-Cola High School sound?

Well, why not? The presence of the soft drink industry has already pervaded our children's lives and education. School districts sign exclusive contracts with beverage companies to earn financial perks, so we've already established that our kids are for sale. To pay for the privilege of being the main supplier of snack and beverage vending machines the cola companies pay districts thousands of dollars a year.

But it's not like we don't know better. When soft drink machines went into schools in the early 1980s we knew it was a bad idea. We knew then that too much sugar and too much caffeine was a lethal combination for kids who were trying to sit still and learn. We knew it wasn't good for their not-yet-fully-grown bodies, too.

But apparently the lure of the almighty dollar is impossible to resist, so we're selling our kids down Willy Wonka's river of sweets.

I've heard experts say that if left to their own devices, kids will usually choose a healthy meal over junk. I don't believe it. I ate lunch in my classroom with high school students every day for eight years, and what they called "lunch" was an assortment of junk that would make you slightly nauseous.

Day after day my lunch bunch came in carrying Doritos, Skittles, chocolate, Honey Buns, and huge bottles of pop. When I incredulously asked if that was really their lunch, they enthusiastically explained that, yeah, they had all the food groups covered: spicy, sour, sweet, and healthy.

"Healthy?" I asked dubiously, eyeing the pile of junk food.

"Yeah, the Honey Buns!" they exclaimed.

Honey Buns? Healthy?

They ravenously wolfed down this "lunch" because most of them didn't eat breakfast. And I only recall two students, *two*, who ever expressed concern about well-balanced meals and made a conscious effort to eat fruits and vegetables.

The number of empty calories my students consumed was staggering. So it's no surprise to me that child obesity has reached epic proportions.

In defense, officials claim that the machines carry "healthy" food, too. But how healthy can it be if it comes from a machine? Even sports drinks and granola bars are full of sugar and preservatives.

I know what school officials are thinking. They're thinking that kids come to them with bad eating habits already, and they're going to eat this stuff anyway, so the district may as well get the revenue and use it for something for the kids. They're also telling themselves that the snacks are for *after* their healthy lunch, not in place of it.

But those excuses aren't good enough. We're making it too easy for children to ruin their health.

Lord knows schools need money. That's the real shame, of course. Government priorities don't include enough funding for education, so school districts are forced to get money where they can.

But is this the best we can do? Where is our vision for the future?

Why wait for the numbers to play out, for this generation to suffer more tooth decay, diabetes, osteoporosis, heart problems, and obesity? Right now, this minute, we can choose to be part of the problem, or part of the solution.

The soda companies love this, though. If the school districts make thousands, imagine how much the soft drink companies make. Plus, they get to shape kids' eating and spending habits, creating lifelong consumers of their products.

It's scary, too, how dependent school districts become on that money. Some incorporate that money into their budget rather than use it for one-shot purchases, and they won't easily give it up.

Lots of schools have vending machine contracts. But as moms everywhere always say, just because everyone else is doing it, doesn't make it right.

Mouse Finger Push-ups

Getting smacked in the eye with a dodge ball is my most vivid memory of gym class. Spending the rest of that day with an ice pack on my face is second. As a ninety-eight-pound weakling I suffered through it all, including being the last one chosen for teams.

I was tense and uncomfortable every minute of every hour of phys. ed. So I empathized mightily when my students complained of their own gym class horrors.

And complain they did. When it came to phys. ed. it seemed that there were two points of view: they loved it, or they hated it. As adviser of the student newspaper most student complaints eventually landed on my desk in the form of letters to the editor. Complaints about having to take phys. ed. were right up there with the condition of the school bathrooms and the quality of the school lunches.

The biggest issue for girls was their hair. They hated arriving at school looking good, only to mess it all up sweating or swimming. And they adamantly maintained that there was not enough time to re-groom and still make it to their next class on time.

They also hated being vulnerable in front of classmates. Embarrassed by their klutziness. Mortified in a swimsuit. So, many simply opted to do the bare minimum, content with a D, as long as they could sit out.

No doubt kids need physical education. But Minneapolis Public Schools offer a brilliant alternative: online physical education classes.

It's a concept that takes some getting used to. How can you take phys. ed. online?

First, kids get to choose their own activity. Competitive Frisbee? No problem. Dance videos? Sure thing. Just about anything goes. Students first meet with a physical education teacher to map out their activity and set goals. Teachers continue to monitor progress with regular check-ins.

Busy kids love the flexibility. They can schedule the activities around their jobs, school, extracurricular activities, and social life. If they want to exercise first thing in the morning, they can. They can also do it right after school, in the evening, or even on the weekend.

It also frees up their schedule for other classes, such as Advanced Placement or electives.

Most important to many kids, though, is that they can do it in the privacy of their own home. No more squirming with embarrassment or feeling like the unhappy center of attention.

What I really love is that it gets kids into the habit of scheduling physical activity into their everyday routines. That's a habit that will serve them well all their lives.

Of course, it's possible that they'll cheat. But then, that's always a possibility, isn't it?

If I'd had the option of taking phys. ed. from home, I would have logged hours waterskiing, bicycling, swimming, ice skating, roller skating, sailing competitively, and cross-country skiing.

But I wouldn't have been dodging balls.

CHAPTER 6

Discipline

IT'S NOT A DIRTY WORD,
IT JUST FEELS LIKE IT

Do You Hang Around
with People Like This?

When it comes to teenagers, adults are so concerned with putting out the big fires like drugs, alcohol abuse, violence, crime, and sex that we're neglecting the small things that make up the fabric of a polite society.

Many offenses that once would have been call-home worthy now fall by the wayside. For example, it's not unusual to hear the "F" word shouted in the halls of a high school. Every day.

Really. Ask a high school teacher. They'll tell you, because they're shocked, too. We used to send kids to the principal's office for swearing, but now, in light of all of the really serious issues that administrators deal with, we are often just told to ask the students to watch their language.

Face it: schools are just a microcosm of society and kids' behavior just reflects what is going on elsewhere in our culture. For this generation TV has been not only the babysitter, but also the role model. You only have to look at a lineup in the *TV Guide* to see that our society is pushing at the boundaries of common sense and good taste all the time. Shows like NBC's *Fear Factor*, and MTV's *Jackass*, *Spring Break* or *Road Rules* applaud bad manners and bad behavior.

I witnessed a revolting example of the decline of polite society at my school while I was monitoring the hall between classes.

I had this sweet freshman student named Josie. Pretty and fresh-faced, endearingly tall and gawky, Josie had a habit of ducking her head and looking shyly up at you from underneath her lashes.

Her boyfriend was a year older, cocky and sure of himself. He had this smart-alecky grin and, as my grandmother would say, "the devil in his eye."

Whenever they were together she was all atwitter and giddy, as if she just couldn't believe her good fortune at having such a catch for a boyfriend.

So I'm standing in the hall, watching the students go by, and here they come with their arms wrapped around each other's waist, pressed against each other all up and down the sides of their bodies. They were sort of turned in at the hip so that they were looking into each other's face. She was staring dreamily into his eyes, and he was grinning that smart-alecky grin back.

So cute. Josie was self-conscious, but proud, hoping that everyone was looking at them and afraid that they might be.

The bell was about to ring so they had to say their good-byes quickly and get to class.

Their faces moved closer together.

Oh, great, I thought. Big kissing scene. I'm going to have to bust them for a Public Display of Affection.

Closer, closer, closer . . .

Just as I was about to move in, the boy, whose face was now about one inch from Josie's, let out an enormous, loud, wet, disgusting burp.

Right into Josie's mouth.

Gasp!

I was so horrified I couldn't speak. My eyes bugged out of my head. I was absolutely riveted by this unbelievable turn of events.

Josie saw me watching and laughed, and tossed her head, and hugged the twerp as if to say, "It's okay, I don't mind, isn't he funny, isn't he wonderful?!"

The boy laughed out loud, smiling his smart-alecky grin. There's no question he did it on purpose.

I know, it's a gross story. My apologies if it shocked you. It shocked me, too. And that's my point. As a high school teacher I witnessed a lot of things that the people I know would never do. But I do know these people. And so do you. These are our people. This is our society.

So why didn't these kids know better? Where did they get the idea that this was acceptable behavior? Why didn't that boy know the proper way to treat a girl? And why didn't Josie value herself enough to know that this was not okay?

We can't sit back and mutter under our breath, "What's wrong with kids today?"

Turn on your TV. Look at what we accept and condone.

The society we have created is what's wrong with kids today.

Discipline? Oh, It's Never Easy

Twenty years in the classroom, and I never once disciplined a student without secretly second-guessing myself and wondering whether I handled it right.

The self-doubt was tormenting. Take, for example, that nonstop talker I moved to three different seats. Did that embarrass her? Or did she love the attention? Could I have teased her into cooperating? Should I have called her mom the very first time she disrupted class? Was I unfair to the quiet kid I put her next to?

And what about that nice boy who had his pocketknife out on his desk? I know he didn't think of it as a weapon. To him, it was just a little pocketknife, like the ones his dad and grandpa carried. But zero tolerance is zero tolerance, and he got expelled. Did I dare look the other way?

Don't get me wrong—I had a reputation for being a fairly strict teacher. My classroom was well managed. And I handled all of my own discipline. I didn't send kids to the office and let someone else dole out the punishment unless the student handbook required me to.

But it was always stressful. Worrying about students' delicate psyches is what keeps teachers lying awake until long past midnight. It's what they think about in the car on the way to school, and on the way home again at night. It's what they talk about—endlessly—to their spouses, and friends, and colleagues in the lounge, looking for advice, or validation. And though they may appear calm and firm in front of their students, behind closed doors they gnash their teeth and worry.

Should I have been tougher on Jason? Easier on Amanda? Have I somehow scarred this child for life? Will this discipline foster a healthy respect? Or will it shut him down so completely that he won't learn anything else all year? Is there a lesson in this discipline? Has she learned it? Or am I just spinning my wheels?

Student behavior is a monstrous issue for school districts. You can't imagine the time and energy that is spent—no, wasted—on student discipline every single day. If you were to wave a magic wand and somehow make all the kids behave, every school would make adequate yearly progress, and teachers would never burn out.

So if your phone rings this marking period, and a school official is on the other end of the line, please know this: That person wants what's best for your child. But she is also responsible for maintaining a positive learning environment for every child.

Trust that she is doing her best to be fair and consistent.

And know that it's never, ever easy.

Life in the Fishbowl

It's not easy to conduct business in a fishbowl. From the outside looking in, things get distorted, refracted, magnified.

That's what happened at Spencer High School in Columbus, Georgia, where seventeen-year-old junior Kevin Francois was suspended for using his cell phone during school hours. The snag in this case was that the student was talking to his mom—a sergeant first class stationed in Iraq.

A teacher saw Francois on the phone and told him to hang up, per school policy. Francois refused and the teacher took him to the office. Allegedly Francois became defiant and used profanity while in the principal's office, earning himself a ten-day suspension.

The court of public opinion deemed that school officials were too hard on Francois, so after receiving hundreds of letters and phone calls, administrators reduced his suspension from ten days to three.

This reflects a disturbing new trend that has students and parents alike second-guessing administrators and campaigning for justice when they feel wronged. How do you think the Spencer High School story made national news? You can bet it wasn't from the school district because discipline records are protected by the Family Educational Rights and Privacy Act.

In schools all across the nation, every minute of every day, school administrators sag under the weight of almost overwhelming discipline problems that have reached epic proportions on the drama scale.

Lunchtime on Fridays at my school were often standing room only in the main office, as kids waited to be disciplined. And our assistant principal spent many mornings sorting out disputes that happened on the buses on the way in that morning.

Principals spend an inordinate amount of time arbitrating discipline. Nothing is black and white, and it takes the wisdom of Solomon to be fair and still maintain a consistent discipline policy.

Too often, what should be a simple discipline decision gets snarled when an angry student with an attitude escalates a simple misunderstanding into a full-blown confrontation.

It's a pretty thankless job to be a principal these days. And it's hard to focus on leadership and teaching and learning while mediating the murky and the absurd.

I'm sure school officials at Spencer High School were chagrined to have this incident make national news. In hindsight, they probably would have handled Francois differently. I've seen school personnel be unbelievably accommodating with families and their personal problems.

But the rules at that school, which were put in place to maintain a studious learning environment and keep kids safe, just took another hit. Once you make an allowance for one student, there's a feeding frenzy as students, and yes, their parents, work every angle.

School discipline used to be about gum chewing or running in the hall. And the student was always guilty, in actuality or not. It may not always have been fair, but at least it was simple.

Things would be much more tolerable in the fishbowl if only people would quit tapping on the glass.

It's the Resistance That Gets to You

Resistance.

That's what makes teaching so gosh-darned hard. A sometimes subtle, sometimes in-your-face resistance that's insidious and unrelenting, making even the simplest tasks gargantuan. And by the end of that first semester, teachers are feeling pretty beat-up.

It's like this. On your way to first hour you see a kid in the hall wearing a cap, a blatant violation of the dress code. You go up to the kid and politely ask him to remove it. Sometimes you're met with a mean glare. Sometimes it escalates into an all-out confrontation, simply because you made an effort to enforce a school rule that has been in place forever. And sometimes they wait until you turn away and put the cap right back on, causing an instant spike to your blood pressure. The halls are full of such rule breakers, but you learn to pick and choose your battles. Who needs unsolicited resistance?

And then there are a dozen daily head-banging conversations like this:

Johnny: "It's not my fault I was late. My ride was late picking me up."

Teacher: "Unless you have a pass in your hand, it's counted as a tardy."

Johnny: "But it's not my fault. My ride was late."

Teacher: "Tardy means you were not here when the last bell rang. That's what tardy is."

Johnny: *"But it's not my fault! My ride was late!"*

There are infinite variations of that theme: *"I shouldn't have to pay for that textbook, it was stolen from me. I had to run full speed through the hall; otherwise I'd be late. I forgot my backpack so I can't do any work. It's not my fault I couldn't do my homework, I wasn't home last night."* And on and on and on.

There's also the resistance you meet when you ask students to do something. Say "Take out your books and turn to page forty," and you're greeted with every sort of sigh, groan, eye-roll, and under-the-breath grumbling: *"Man, this is so boring, why do we always have to do work, why can't school be fun, all we ever do is work, I'm too tired, I hate this class, man, this sucks!"*

They resist responsibility, too. Their grade is never their fault. No matter how little work they've done, or what the grade book shows in black and white, a low grade is always because the teacher doesn't like them.

It's like swimming up a waterfall. By the end of the day you're tapped out, bone tired from fighting against all of that resistance.

But if resistance is the disease, tenacity is the cure. Resistance doesn't stand a chance, because there's no more tenacious person on earth than a teacher.

And besides, at the end of the day, all it takes is one friendly student to pop her head in and say, "See you tomorrow, Ms. Flynn!"

And you smile in anticipation.

Take Back the Halls

I can tell you how to improve every school in this country in four words: Take back the halls.

In some schools, on some days, the general public would be shocked at how students behave in the halls between classes. While many move peacefully, minding their own business, far too many think hall time is party time, and that hall behavior has nothing to do with classroom behavior. Simple requests to stop running, remove hats, put away cell phones, or stop swearing are greeted with a "make me" attitude, which is second only to the "you can't make me" attitude.

But school officials at Morton High School in Hammond, Indiana, finally had enough. On the very first day of school, within minutes of opening the doors, they suspended 128 students—ten percent of the 1,200 student body—for dressing inappropriately and for cell phone use.

School officials, with school board support, sent a loud, clear message that they would not tolerate dress code violations. They told students they would remove the infraction from their records in twelve weeks if they had no other in-school violations.

If school rules are enforced haphazardly—and believe me, they are—it sends the message that those rules are not important. But if the goal is teaching and learning, the learning environment must be sacred. Teachers, administrators—and parents—must insist on it.

It happens in every school: teachers and administrators alike often look the other way if they're too busy or too tired to enforce a rule. I remember well how frustrating it was to watch a student carrying a soft drink or wearing a hat, walk right past a principal, or another teacher.

I once came upon a girl and a boy standing outside my classroom door with their tongues stretched far out of their mouths, rubbing them together. I was horrified. Believe me, more than anything I wanted to turn on my heel and pretend I didn't see it. It would have been far easier. Instead I issued a reprimand and endured their rolled eyes, heavy sighs, and snide mutterings.

If kids run wild in the halls, it's the adults who are to blame. A well-disciplined school is a choice. The choice is not made by the students, but by the adults in charge of those students. Face it, it's far easier to take the easy way out and pretend you don't see something than to go to the trouble to deal with it.

The entire country is focused on higher standards in education. But that focus is largely trained on test scores.

If we want students to take education seriously, educators must start by insisting that the learning environment be respected. And parents need to step up to the plate and support that, too.

The place to start is in the halls.

To Suspend . . .

"I know, I can't do anything with him at home, either."

You can't imagine how many times I heard those words when I called a parent to discuss a student's misbehavior in class. The subtext? "You're on your own."

And yet, in an infuriating irony, schools face derision for suspending too many rude, disruptive, violent children, whose parents consider the public school system as nothing more than a free babysitting service.

You only have to watch five minutes of the television show *Supernanny* to know what kids I'm talking about. Record numbers of parents have no control over their children, yet camouflage their parental inadequacy by pointing the finger at someone else—namely, the public school that has the gall to say "your bad behavior is not welcome here."

But before you point that finger, think about this: when school personnel are forced to spend an inordinate amount of time dealing with your defiant child, they are cheating dozens of other children out of meaningful, positive interactions.

And that is why schools suspend students. Few discipline options are left. Heck, they can't even make students wash desks when they're caught writing on them because it might damage their fragile little psyches.

If a student is suspended for something seemingly trivial, such as disrupting class, most likely it was several days of disrupting class that resulted in that referral to the office. And often students are suspended for their *response* to a reprimand. For example, a student probably won't be suspended for turning around in his seat during a lesson. But if you ask him to face front and pay attention, and he responds with "Fuck off" he will be suspended for that.

Things like peer mediation, anger counseling, and restorative justice are fine and dandy, but if parents were doing their job, school districts would not have to spend time and money on the facility, staff, and training necessary to implement those programs.

Let's put the blame back in its rightful place. It's the parents. It's always the parents. If you don't teach your child the meaning of the word "no," if you send your child to school believing that he does not have to follow rules, if he does not know how to share and play fair and be quiet when someone else is talking, then do not be surprised when you eventually get a call because your child has been suspended. You have not done your job to ensure that your child knows how to function in society.

We can't have it both ways. We cannot require schools to raise academic standards and achievement, but expect them to do it with troublemakers in the classroom.

As a country we need to decide: Do we want schools to be in the business of teaching and learning? Or do we want schools to be in the business of social work?

They don't have the resources to do both.

Or Not to Suspend?

Suspending students from school is a crappy discipline tactic. Don't think for a minute that school personnel don't know it. They know it's illogical to suspend a kid for skipping. They know it's senseless to suspend a kid all day, when he misbehaved in one class. They know that kids purposely work the suspension system to get time off.

They know all of that. They're just hard-pressed for options. Alternatives cost money, and there's never enough of that.

You need to know, though, that most public schools are not full of out-of-control students. Most classes on most days run smoothly. A lot of learning takes place.

But I'd be lying if I didn't acknowledge that the number of, and severity of, discipline problems has increased, while punishment options have decreased.

The "Yeah? What you gonna do about it?" kids are the worst. No matter how offensive their behavior, they know you can't touch, embarrass, humiliate, or offend them, so they challenge you. Once they have that attitude, forget it. You might as well suspend them, because they'll be insufferable. We're glad to see those kids go.

But for most infractions by basically good kids, suspension is a bad option. They get behind on their schoolwork, but worse, they have too much fun at home. An astounding number of parents do not reinforce a suspension punishment, and allow kids to sleep, watch television, and play video games all day. It's beyond aggravating when a kid returns from suspension bragging about the fun he had.

Many years ago my district had an in-school suspension program. For two years my husband was the teacher who ran it. And though he's a kind man with a good sense of humor, kids did *not* want to end up in that room. It was not fun. If they said they had no schoolwork he provided plenty, and made sure they did it. They were completely isolated from their friends. No sleeping. No talking.

When money got tight the in-school suspension program was cut. A few years later, a Saturday detention was implemented. Kids slept, played cards, ate, drank pop, talked, and hung out with friends in the cafeteria. True, they did have to give up a Saturday, but all in all, as punishment goes, it was pretty fun.

The intention of both programs was punishment with no missed school. But any program is only as effective as the person in charge of it.

And a good program costs money. It requires a classroom, preferably off the beaten path—not easy to come by in crowded schools where every room is in use every hour. And it requires trained staff—preferably a teacher—to assign, and help with, schoolwork.

Ideally, every school would have an in-school suspension program for disruptive students.

And, in a perfect world, districts would have the power to make their parents sit right there next to them.

"Is Tardy the Same as Late?"

Were you late for work this week? Was your child late for school?

One of the most exasperating issues teachers deal with daily is student tardiness. I'll bet, though, that most parents have no idea how disruptive tardiness is, not only to their child's education, but to the rest of the class, too.

Picture this: The bell rings, kids are seated, teacher takes roll, logs it into the computer, and begins class. She's got their attention, the lesson is rolling along, and five minutes later, bang! goes the door and in strolls Johnny. All heads turn to look, concentration broken. Teacher must stop the lesson, note the time, log back in, and change Johnny's absence to a tardy, lest the record be inaccurate.

"So, what are we doing?" Johnny asks, and again teacher stops, this time to fill him in. Meanwhile, the rest of the class waits. If another student comes in late, they wait some more. Johnny has missed announcements, the lesson introduction, and the accompanying student questions, so he starts class confused and behind.

For a parent or a student, the occasional tardy may seem inconsequential. But the cumulative effect for the teacher, who may have two to three tardy students each hour, is the stuff migraines are made of.

This is not just a high school problem. This disregard for punctuality starts at the elementary level and is taught and encouraged by parents. Elementary teachers tell me that often they can't teach the first and last half hours of the day, because so many parents drop off and pick up their kids at their own convenience.

These parents give lots of reasons for ignoring the school schedule: they want to beat the busses, they have other children to pick up or drop off, it suits *their* schedule, they overslept. It's always disruptive because once the first parent arrives, the rest of the kids see it as the end of their school day, too, their minds turning to their own freedom.

The lack of respect for the school schedule trickles down to the child, resulting in disrespect for education in general, and a disregard for the sanctity of the classroom specifically.

The second part of the equation is the attitude that comes with the tardy. High school students think that if they're late for a "real" reason, like a flat tire, they're not really late. And they'll vehemently defend their lateness with, "It's not my fault!" followed by "I'm not responsible for this information—I wasn't here!"

High school tardy policies always allow for a few real emergencies. But teens think they can use those for dawdling at the drinking fountain, and tardies beyond their control should go unpunished. How do you teach them that tardy is tardy, when their parents have taught them it's not?

Parents hold the key to teaching the importance of punctuality.

When it comes to being late, if you're living it, they're learning it.

This Isn't a Correspondence Course, You Know

Okay, folks, we can't teach them if they aren't here.

Student attendance. It can make or break your child's education. And unfortunately, it absolutely consumes the time of teachers, principals, and secretaries, compromising the efficiency of the entire staff in our constant chase to play catch-up with absent kids.

Let me be clear: I'm not talking about absenteeism due to legitimate illness. School personnel are happy to work with parents and students there. And I know there are many kids with good attendance.

But I also know that the attendance problem is getting worse, not better. To some, school is merely a correspondence course, where they drop in occasionally to pick up assignments.

The weird thing is how many parents work the scam, too. Instead of setting a good example and backing the attendance policy set by the school district, too many parents join their kids in looking for every loophole.

But it's the trivial reasons kids miss school that really floor me.

A student once told me she didn't come to school because the rain would mess up her hair. Another told me she didn't come because she didn't have time to wash her hair. "I overslept" is a universal excuse, but one that kids believe to be perfectly legitimate. Some miss the bus and have no other way to get to school. Others are just too cool to ride the bus, and won't come if they can't get a ride. Many stay home to babysit younger siblings.

A colleague told me that she once had a parent call a kid in sick while the kid was sitting in class. He hadn't gone home the night before, and instead of worrying about that, Mom was covering for him. Another colleague told me that a student missed school to attend a party for her grandpa who was just released from prison. I wish I were kidding, but I'm not.

State requirements have upped the ante on documentation. Gone are the days when we scrawled the names of absent students on a slip of paper and clipped it to the door. Attendance policies have become a fine art as schools strive for the right balance between accountability and fairness, in a policy that is clear and easy to follow, with minimal paperwork for all.

Teachers from all over have shared with me the attendance policies at their school. Mind-boggling paperwork can require signatures in triplicate of all involved parties, complicated forms, and elaborate appeals processes.

But documentation is only half the problem. Providing students with material they missed is almost a full-time job in itself. And truly, spending half an hour on make-up work for a student who stayed home to watch a wedding on *All My Children* exasperates even the most patient teacher.

And as with many things, it's the cumulative effect that takes its toll. If it had only been one or two kids a day, it wouldn't have been as frustrating. But often it was three or four an hour who missed class for no good reason. That added up to twelve to fifteen absent kids per day.

Don't get me wrong. Most teachers are more than willing to go all out to help a kid with a legitimate excuse for being absent, often tutoring them at lunch or after school.

But think about it. How do you catch up a kid who has missed an entire lecture, or a class discussion, or a lab? You can't re-create the entire lesson after the fact and maintain the integrity of it, with all of its subtle nuances. And if she missed a quiz or a test, a make-up session had to be scheduled after school or at lunch, often with a different version of the test to make sure there was no cheating.

Sometimes attendance policies make it seem like we spend more time on the kids we didn't teach than the ones we did.

And I swear if it hadn't been for the insanity of the attendance policy of 1999, I might still be teaching.

The Honeymoon Is Just Too Darn Short

The honeymoon is over.

Actually, honeymoons aren't what they used to be. The honeymoon for teachers is that first few weeks of school when the kids are on their very best behavior, when they wear their new school clothes, bring all of their bright and shiny school supplies, and answer politely when spoken to.

But the honeymoon seems to get shorter every year. Now it's more like a night at Motel 6 than two weeks at Club Med.

In some classes, there isn't a honeymoon at all. A few years ago one of my Beginning Journalism classes burst into the room on the first day of school, started talking, and didn't stop.

Ever.

"Hey, what's going on with these freshmen?" exclaimed Kirstie, my senior student assistant. "Aren't they supposed to be nice for at least a few days?" she asked. "They act like this is the last day of school, not the first."

The honeymoon lasted much, much longer when I first started teaching. A teacher could always count on at least a month of good behavior from the students. But years of having free reign at home has made many kids think that they have free reign at school, too.

For some, the honeymoon ends when interim reports go home. Most schools send interim reports of some kind halfway through the marking period. (Parents, it would be a good idea if you got to the mailbox first. And remind your child that tampering with the U.S. mail is a federal offense.)

Some parents get a rude awakening when they realize that their child is not telling them what's really going on in class. The interim report sounds the alarm. It's not a recorded grade that goes on transcripts, but merely a communication to parents and students about how they're doing so far.

I think the biggest surprise for parents is that their kid isn't turning in assignments.

"I don't get it," they'll say to Johnny. "I bought $100 worth of school supplies last month and you haven't turned in sixteen assignments?"

In the next breath they'll turn to the teacher and say, "But I always ask Johnny if he has any homework, and he always says 'No.'" (It's amazing that so many parents admit this.)

How can I say this politely?

Johnny is lying.

And the fact that he is lying is a personal problem, not the teacher's problem, so parents shouldn't expect the teacher to solve it. (And aren't you embarrassed that you haven't made it your business to know?)

Parents shouldn't expect the teacher to call every time a child misses an assignment, either. Do the math; a parent has one (or two, or three) children. The teacher has as many as 150. A parent lives with the child. The child's teacher sees him for about fifty-five minutes per day, and those fifty-five minutes are shared with approximately thirty other kids. A parent has known the child all of his life—the child's teacher really barely knows him and won't know him well for a while.

By sending interim reports schools are communicating grade information to parents every four to five weeks. That's eight times a year. In between, parents need to do their part. There's plenty of time to correct poor study habits and raise those grades before the first report card.

The honeymoon for teachers is much too short.

When that interim report gets home, it may be over for Johnny, too.

Spoiled Athletes Can Rot School Policies

Doesn't surprise me a bit that pro athletes think the world revolves around them. Why wouldn't they? It has since they first picked up a ball and ran with it.

No doubt about it, we live in a sports crazy culture. Athletes get all kinds of special treatment. Favors are granted. They're bailed out of trouble. Bad behavior is excused. They are idolized beyond all reason. Pro athletes get away with murder.

And it all starts in high school.

All kinds of allowances are made for high school athletes, every day. Infractions of school rules are ignored, teachers are pressured, grades get changed.

It's wrong. It's unfair. And it's true.

I once had a young star athlete come ten to fifteen minutes late to my class fourteen times in nine weeks. In the middle of my lesson he'd stroll in, carrying a pass from the principal. He would take his time getting to his chair, look around the room, then look at me and say, "So, what are we doing?" Office workers told me that he and the principal were simply sitting in the office talking sports every day.

Every school has an academic eligibility policy. Some are more strict than others. But the policy is only as strong as the people who enforce it. The easiest way around it is to pressure the classroom teacher into making allowances for the athlete. I've had coaches, parents, and even principals knock on my door in the middle of my class to find out what a particular athlete could do to pass. "C'mon," they'll ask, "can't he just do a report or something?"

When a kid isn't eligible to play his sport, some parents would rather blame anyone but their child. The child can have ten assignments not turned in and the parents will call it a "personality conflict" with the teacher. Sometimes they demand, and get, a class change to a different (i.e., easier) teacher past the deadline for class changes. Other students don't get that privilege. Sometimes parents resort to begging, using guilt about that child's future to pressure the teacher.

Some teachers won't give in, and choose to keep their standards high. Ironically, these teachers are often labeled "spoilsports" or considered not to be team players. Their school spirit is questioned. If they're female, they're dubbed "old biddies."

If parents can't change the teacher, they might go after the eligibility policy itself. In my school district we had an efficient, computerized eligibility procedure in place. Each week teachers were given a list of athletes who were in their particular classes. With a minimum of fuss, a teacher could figure each athlete's cumulative GPA, and simply check off whether they were failing or near failing. It was fast and easy.

We had a particularly outstanding athlete who was placed on the near failing list several times. Just before a big game when college scouts would be in attendance he fell to the failing list. He claimed that he had no idea he was failing, even though his teachers had been following procedure.

His parents claimed he didn't know. They called central administration and voila! Suddenly we had a whole new step to add to our system. Now teachers had to take the list around to each athlete and get their signature to prove that they were told that they were on it.

Even though he was failing, we let him play in that game. And the message we sent to the entire student body was, "If you're special, the rules will be rearranged for you." This angers the "ordinary" kids, because they know that they won't likely receive such favoritism.

Why do we feel compelled to bend all the rules for gifted athletes? Why do we put them on a pedestal? After all, it's not as if the world couldn't get along without sports.

Maybe it's unrealistic to expect a school not to reflect society's love of sports and athletes.

But must we be accomplices in creating athletes without character?

Follow the Rules, Make the News

I'm still an English teacher at heart, so I'm always looking for a really good example of irony, something that my students can relate to.

This story about a football championship at a small Catholic school in Alton, Illinois, is a perfect example of irony.

After twenty years of unremarkable football teams, the Marquette Explorers finally went 10–0 and made it to the championship playoffs. Then sixteen starters, including the coach's son, were arrested for underage drinking at a party, and, in compliance with school policy, were benched for the playoff game.

According to Principal John Rogers, and Coach Mike Slaughter, there was no debate about allowing the students to serve their punishment in another way.

Sounds simple, doesn't it? Here's the rule, here's the penalty for breaking the rule. The kids broke the rule, now they serve the punishment.

Unfortunately, in our pass-the-buck, take-no-blame society, parents often do their kids a huge disservice by insisting that they be the exception to the rule.

And because kids learn more by the example we set than they ever do by what we say, we're raising a generation of kids who think the challenge is to see what they can get away with.

It's refreshing, then, that in a culture that idolizes athletes and pays homage to sports, these school officials did the right thing, and better yet, the parents supported them.

Every day in schools everywhere, administrators do the right thing and stand up to parental pressure.

And sometimes they don't.

I have been pressured by a principal who was being pressured by parents. It's not pretty.

Against my better judgment, I used the student bathroom once and accidentally caught a girl smoking. I took her to the office, wrote up the requisite discipline form, and left. Two hours later the principal was at my classroom door.

"Did you actually see her put the cigarette to her mouth?" he asked.

"Well, I saw her hand moving *away* from her mouth, and her hand was holding a lit cigarette," I said.

"But did you actually *see* her inhale?" he asked.

"I don't know," I said. "I don't smoke. But it certainly *looked* like she had just inhaled. Smoke came out of her mouth."

"So you didn't really see her inhale, then," he said. "Maybe it wasn't her cigarette."

"There was only one other person in there," I said, "and she was in a stall."

"Ah," he said. "So it could have been the other girl's cigarette."

The point of this ugly conversation is, of course, that parental pressure happens even when championship games are not at stake.

That's what makes the story about Marquette so ironic. Rogers and Slaughters simply followed the rules, yet their story was picked up by the national wire service and made the front page of the newspaper.

They were heralded as heroes simply because they followed the rules.

They could have found a way around it. They could have let the kids play the championship game. They might have won, too, but it would have been a hollow victory.

The second and third strings were given a standing ovation at the end of the game, in spite of a 63–0 loss. But because of the fine example set by Rogers, Slaughter, and the parents of this community, they won a victory of gigantic proportions.

The adults in their lives honored the system they put into place and in doing so set an example those kids will never forget.

CHAPTER 7

Parents
YOU DIDN'T THINK THE CLIENT WAS THE STUDENT, DID YOU?

Parent–Teacher Conferences Provide Enlightenment

When parents sit down across from me at parent–teacher conferences, everything I've ever wondered about a kid suddenly becomes crystal clear. Talk about a learning experience . . .

THE BULLY

These parents bully the student right in front of me, demanding that the student account for the grade. Sometimes they are quite belligerent. The student often lies about why the grade is so low and I'm left to decide how much to rat on the kid. I can tell all, or help the kid out and hold something back. Sometimes if I hold something back the kid is grateful and will make an effort to be better next time. I always wonder and worry about what happens when these families get home.

THE THREE RING CIRCUS

These parents makes a big show of being tough with the kid, the kid argues back and none of them listens to a word I say. One parent asks a question, I start to answer, the kid interrupts me and makes excuses about his grade. Pretty soon he has successfully diverted the parents' attention and they're off, arguing about everything. I watch for a while and then they leave. I always feel slightly used after an encounter like this, as if I've merely provided a backdrop for their drama.

THE PERFECTIONIST

Some parents will grill me about why their child got an A–. I've even had these parents ask me to tutor their child after school. Often, but not always, these parents are Asian or Indian. They will shake their head, wrinkle their brow, and mutter under their breath that an A– is not acceptable. I'm never sure if they are upset with me, or the child, but that student always raised that A– to an A by the next marking period.

THE SHY

Shy parents come in, sit down, and squirm uncomfortably. They don't ask questions and seem to be there because they think they should be, as if they read it in some parenting handbook, but didn't quite understand the chapter. I tell them a little bit about the class, the work, their child's performance, and then ask if they have any questions. They usually don't. They don't know when to leave and seem to wait to be excused.

THE BLAMER

These parents blame everything and everybody except their own child for their kid's performance. They grill you, looking for a loophole, a chink in your armor, a weakness in your teaching methods or your grading system, something they can pounce on. You learn very quickly with these parents not to volunteer any information and to keep your answers short and to the point. Above all, keep your voice neutral and your face expressionless, lest they take offense to your tone or manner. These are the parents that teach you the importance of documentation and you quickly learn to document every conversation you have with them, or their child, to save your hide lest you find yourself in court. You dodge and sprint fast as a quarterback to get away if you see them in public. I once ducked behind a display of purses at Target to hide from one of these parents.

THE APATHETIC

This is a typical conversation with an apathetic girl and her bewildered mother:

> Mother: (*bewildered*) "I don't know why Susie has such a low grade. She never brings any homework home."
> Me: "Well, Susie didn't do twenty-one assignments, and these weren't even for homework, these exercises were done in class."
> Mother: (*turns to daughter, clearly perplexed*) "Why didn't you turn them in?"
> Daughter: (*sullen, won't meet her mother's eyes or mine, shrugs*)
> Mother: "Well, why don't you do the assignments if you have plenty of time in class?"
> Daughter: (*shrugs again, this time turning head away and looking very bored, stares off into space*)
> Mother: (*looks at me helplessly*)
> Me: "Susie, why don't you do the work?"
> Daughter: (*shrugs again, squirms a little*)
> Me: "Is the work too difficult for you?"
> Daughter: "No."
> Me: "I don't think it is either. You're a bright girl and you should be acing this class."
> Daughter: (*no response*)

Mother nags a little more, daughter refuses to respond, rolls her eyes a few times, looks like she can't stand her mother. (At this point, neither can I). Mother gives up easily, states several times that she doesn't know what to do, and eventually the apathetic pair leaves with nothing resolved.

THE SUPPORTIVE

Supportive parents are surprisingly few and far between, but they are a breath of fresh air. These are the parents who are interested in the curriculum, interested to know what their child's strengths and weaknesses are, and who are supportive of the teacher and the school system. These are the parents that you keep in touch with after their child is out of your class, parents that you are happy to run into in the grocery store or mall. They love their kids unconditionally, but they are savvy enough to know that kids will be kids and even theirs aren't perfect. They take this with a grain of salt and a sense of humor. They keep an open mind and they realize that by treating teachers with respect, they teach their children the most important lesson of all: to value education.

So, Can You Handle the Truth?

Do you know what your teenager is up to?

Are you sure?

If you think so, perhaps you should see the movie *Thirteen* written by director Catherine Hardwicke and fifteen-year-old Nikki Reed (who also stars in the movie). It depicts the subculture of the world of teens, specifically two thirteen-year-old girls who fall into drugs and sex in their desperation to be popular.

This movie will shock you. It will also make you wistful for the good old days, when thirteen-year-old girls played 45s and watched *American Bandstand*. And it will show you the ease with which teenagers can deceive parents who allow themselves to be deceived.

You'll wonder why these parents didn't know what their kids were up to. If they live in the same house, how could the parents be so easily duped?

After twenty years of teaching teens I think I know the answer. Parents don't know because they don't want to know. They may acknowledge that teens do drugs and have sex, but they don't believe that their kids do drugs and have sex.

Our culture is letting teenagers down by looking the other way, by stepping back when we should be stepping in. But it's not just parents who are letting kids down. Adults in general are letting kids down, too.

I heard and saw a lot of what my students were up to, but I learned early in my career to be very careful about what I told parents. Because parents have no qualms about shooting the messenger when confronted with things they don't want to know.

My first year in the classroom I happened to intercept a note that was being passed by a freshman boy. In it he described in great detail the drugs he had used at a party the previous weekend.

I went to my principal for advice. She said my first mistake was reading the note, because once you read them, you can't ignore what's in them. Now I had to call the boy's mother.

I called and asked her to pick up the note. She arrived, read it, and then huffily told me she would talk to her son about it. She called me the next day and said that her son explained the whole thing, and that it was just a big misunderstanding. He didn't really use the drugs. She was very, very angry with me for insinuating such a thing, as was her son.

I continued to see and hear evidence of his drug use, but short of catching him red-handed, there was no more I could do. I certainly never shared my concerns with his mother again.

I never read another note passed by a student again, either.

Another time I watched as one of my very nice, polite female students got pulled under the spell of an older, faster, mean girl. Soon, the nice girl started behaving badly, too. I had met the younger girl's mother at conferences, so I called her to share my observations. The first thing she wanted to know, of course, was who the older girl was. I figured that if it were me I would want to know, too, so I told her.

She talked with her daughter and told her what I said. The younger girl told the older girl, the older girl told *her* mom, and soon the older girl's mom called, accusing me of bad-mouthing her daughter.

It's a dilemma teachers face all the time as they walk the line of political correctness. We know which kids are trouble, but we can't say which kids are trouble.

If a teacher sees a student in immediate danger, say physically abused or suicidal, we will, of course, follow the appropriate procedure. But there's a whole lot that we see that you're not going to hear about.

Do your teen's teachers know more about what he or she is up to than you do? It's possible. Are they going to tell you? Maybe. Maybe not.

It depends on whether you're willing to hear it.

I'm Watching You

Apparently Big Brother is not the only one who's watching.

Mom and Dad are watching, too.

James Bond-like surveillance equipment is now de rigueur at electronics and home improvement stores, and it's being touted as a way to keep tabs on your teenagers. It's also surprisingly affordable.

Pity. After years of letting the TV set babysit our kids, now we're letting surveillance equipment do it.

But hi-tech equipment can't take the place of a real, live parent.

Teenagers need guidance. One on one. They need to know that the adults in their lives are going to be there, in their business, every time they turn around.

As a high school teacher I certainly met many wonderful, involved parents, people who could write books on good parenting. Unfortunately, there were far too many absent parents. It was not unusual for me to spend over a week trying to reach a parent by phone, even if I left a message every single day.

If you want to know what your kids are up to, you need to be where they are. So I always appreciated some of the creative, hands-on approaches the parents of some of my students had.

For example, Jamal had a serious tardy problem. He just couldn't get to class on time. His dad, bless his heart, decided that he wanted to see *why* Jamal couldn't get to class on time, so he came to school and escorted him to all six of his classes.

This poor dad worked nights, but he sat in the back of every one of Jamal's classes that day, struggling to keep his eyes open. It worked, though. Jamal got the message, loud and clear. If he couldn't make it to class on time, Dad was going to make it his business to know why.

I had a student named Jeff who just wouldn't pay attention in class. He was also disruptive and rude. I described his behavior to his father and then invited him in to see for himself.

When Jeff's dad walked into my third hour class and sat down, the kids whispered and pointed. When unsuspecting Jeff walked in and saw his dad sitting there, he turned five shades of red before he reached his seat.

Needless to say, Jeff didn't act up that day. In fact, he didn't act up again. Just knowing that his dad *might* show up was enough to keep him in line.

A colleague told me a similar story. Unbeknownst to Joe, his dad showed up at the end of sixth hour and asked this teacher if he could wait in the hall for his son. When the bell rang kids poured out of the classroom, and there was Dad waiting for Joe. A loud conversation ensued drawing the teacher to the door to make sure everything was okay.

"What the *heck* is you doin' with yo' pants down 'round yo' butt like that?" the dad hollered.

"I done tol' you and tol' you, no son of mine is gonna walk 'round in public with his pants down below his butt. You get them pants, up, son, I'm telling you, right now. You don't gotta belt, I git you some rope, but you gonna get them pants up *now!*"

Apparently Joe and his dad had had this conversation before.

You want to know what your kids are up to?

Be there.

Parental Harassment Can Really Zap Your Zest for Teaching

The first year I taught, a friend told me that teachers weren't really professionals because they belonged to a union. That was news to me. I was so green I wasn't even aware I was in a union. As a typically overwhelmed first year teacher, if it wasn't happening in my classroom, it wasn't of interest to me.

Eventually that changed though, and I did my stint in my local education association, holding various positions. And while I haven't always agreed with the union, I wouldn't want to set foot in a classroom without it. Over the years I learned how vital its protection is. In a profession where every move you make and every word you utter is closely scrutinized, the union offers some protection against vindictive, unstable parents and students.

When I left education I packed up twenty years' worth of classroom memories and materials. Looking through a file cabinet while cleaning the basement, I came across something that still, thirteen years later, had the ability to make my stomach clench. There, sinister as a scorpion, was the inch-thick Harrington file.

Duane Harrington was a student in my freshman English class. He was an average student whose motivation for schoolwork came in haphazard bursts. He was a nice kid, reasonably polite and well behaved. I liked him.

The one thing that made Duane really stand out, though, was his unfortunate ability to somehow end up with all of the worst teachers on the staff.

At least, that's how his mother saw it.

For one solid year, Mrs. Harrington made me, and five of my colleagues, absolutely miserable. For reasons unknown to us she had a chip on her shoulder the size of a boulder. A master manipulator, she tape-recorded our phone conversations with her and then used our words against us.

If Duane earned a C, she insisted that he was gifted, absolutely not a C student. She regularly pressured all of us to change his grades.

Grading his papers was torture. Did I dare write a comment on it? If I said it was "good," she would demand to know why I didn't write more. If I wrote more, she would demand to know why I was picking on him. She was an extremely angry woman, and she took it out on us.

Harassment like that takes a huge toll on teachers, who pride themselves on professionalism and fairness. It's not easily shrugged off, even if the harasser *is* unstable. I can't tell you how many nights' sleep I lost over her.

As a public servant you answer to many bosses: the students, their parents, administrators, school board members, taxpayers. There aren't many professions that leave you as vulnerable.

That she so rabidly condemned all six of us ultimately weakened her case. If it had been just one of us, though, she could have seriously damaged our professional reputation.

Though Mrs. Harrington almost gave me an ulcer that year, I learned a valuable tool that served me well over the years: documentation. I bought a planner, and every time I spoke to her I wrote down the date, time, place, and a synopsis of the conversation. I was armed and ready every time she tried to twist my words.

I still have my planner archives, containing the time-consuming documentation of hundreds of conversations with parents. Precious time I could have spent with students.

The teachers' union gets a bum rap for protecting bad teachers. Unfortunately, there's incompetence in every profession: doctors, lawyers, cops.

But in my experience, the union protects far more top-notch teachers than poor ones. I can think of three times in my career when a teacher did something inappropriate and was terminated immediately. I can think of many more times, though, when the union aided good teachers who were being hunted like witches and harassed until their hair turned gray and the zest for teaching was sucked right out of them.

I held onto the Harrington file all those years because of my irrational fear of a lawsuit.

It's now nothing but shreds buried in the local landfill.

Hovercrafts Need to Take Off

Oh, it's a love/hate relationship teachers have with their students' parents, no doubt about it.

But with problem parents, the verdict is out on which parent is worse: the absent parent that can't be reached by phone and never comes to conferences, or the "hovercrafts," that new breed of parent who is umbilically, weirdly, voraciously, obsessively, neurotically overinvolved with their kids.

It's become such an issue that some schools have added rules to their handbooks, stipulating the appropriate extent of parental involvement. Websites are devoted to teaching parents how to let go. Some colleges are even addressing the issue at freshman orientation.

I once had a mom demand (not ask) that I send her a signed note describing the day's assignment, whether her daughter did it, the quality of the work, and her classroom behavior—*every single day*. (Imagine if all 140 parents wanted me to do that.) The girl was a freshman who earned mostly Bs and Cs.

I complied because, believe it or not, it was easier than arguing with her. I knew she would never see it from my perspective, that she was cheating her daughter out of an important learning experience. There were several other processes already in place for students to keep track of their own assignments—processes designed to teach them personal responsibility.

That's the thing about overinvolved parents—they are unwilling to let their child assume responsibility for his or her own actions. They want to orchestrate their child's world and in the school system, they usually can. But what happens when that child goes out into a world that doesn't dance to mom and dad's tune?

Hovercraft parents also believe that they are the only ones who have their child's best interests at heart. That's not true, of course, but it often puts them at odds with the other adults in the child's life.

What's more, they can't imagine that you could know anything about their child that they don't know. But we do. We see your kids in a completely different context than you do. That can reveal some very cool things about a kid—and some not so cool, which hovercraft parents do not believe anyway.

I'm not advocating parental neglect. Goodness knows we see too much of that. And teachers do want open communication with parents.

The problem with hovercrafts is that they they're hovering so close they lose sight of the big picture: that the most essential lesson a parent can teach a child is self-sufficiency.

Work That System, Baby

If you're not getting everything you want from the public school system, you're just not trying.

Because believe me, some parents are. Some parents work the system like pros. They get the teachers they want, they get the classes they want, and all too often they get the discipline they want. Some even get curriculum changed the way they want it.

Don't get me wrong—parental involvement is not a bad thing. It's a good thing. But it's interesting to note how really clever, even downright diabolical, some parents are at getting what they want, while other parents remain clueless about the power they hold.

One year we had a really screwy attendance policy at my school. As a result, come June, dozens of seniors were going to fail. It was painful. The majority of parents managed to get their kids off so they could graduate, while those with less savvy parents didn't get to walk on graduation night. It was flat out unfair all the way around.

It was a rotten message to send to the absent students, too; attendance is not important, and your parents will bail you out of trouble. But it was terribly distressing to watch only a few take the punishment that all deserved.

And that's the rub when parents figure out ways around the rules. There's nothing wrong with looking out for your child's interests. Yet it's so unfair to the ones who don't have parents who advocate for them.

I'm not saying that school districts shouldn't be receptive to their clientele. Of course they should. In fact, smart school officials work with this parental phenomenon, instead of against it. They cultivate parental involvement, and channel it where they need it most. Smart school officials know that everyone is more cooperative if they feel some ownership in the proceedings.

Smart school officials also communicate clearly and often with parents, because nothing makes a parent more ornery than feeling like information is being withheld from them, or that policies are being sprung on them.

But school officials walk a fine line. They must hold a vision of the big picture, but still appease individuals. They need to recognize self-serving parental intentions and respond to them in the context of what's best for all.

Parents walk a fine line, too. Look out for your kid, but pay attention to the lesson your advocacy teaches.

Our school was not unique in this. Every school system, public or private, has parents who work the system and get unfair advantages. And it's not just schools; in society, rules are finessed every day.

The squeaky wheel really does get the grease. So if you're not a power player in your child's public school experience, get crackin'. Just make sure you use your powers for good.

And not evil.

It's the Little Things That Get in the Way

I was sitting in a restaurant last spring when a lady at the next table asked the waitress for a pencil. Her son, she said, needed to do his homework.

I watched the child push plates and glasses aside to make a little room on the table for his paper, while the adults around him laughed and talked and drank their beer. The child was drinking a Coke.

And while I had to give that mom points for making sure the homework got done, I also wondered why the child was out so late on a school night, and why he was drinking caffeine at bedtime.

I had dozens of conversations with my own students about their lives outside of school, and I learned that there are all sorts of things that impede learning. For example, kids routinely reported that they could not do their homework because they were not at home the night before. They offered this up matter-of-factly, believing themselves blameless because of it.

And perhaps they were. After all, how could they do homework if they spent the evening trapped in the car, being dragged to the laundromat, the bank, and half a dozen stores, visiting friends and relatives, stopping here to drop off this and there to pick up that?

Sometimes it took me weeks to get a hold of a parent, leaving message after message in a house where no one was home.

Lack of sleep is a huge problem, too. I was surprised at how many students told me they *couldn't* sleep, and yet they drank caffeinated beverages all day.

It's important to note that I'm not talking about children who are overscheduled in organized activities like gymnastics, soccer, and dance. I'm talking about the trivial busyness that keeps some families running all the time.

Don't get me wrong—these are not bad parents. The worst that can be said is that they are, perhaps, unfocused, overbooked, and disorganized. The problem is that kids get too used to the busyness, never learn how to fill their own time, and become easily bored when there is no outside stimulus to entertain them.

Teachers are aware of dozens of such impediments to learning, seemingly insignificant, yet insidious things that are too intangible to be quantified and measured.

And because they haven't been quantified and measured they will never be cited as a cause for low test scores or bad grades. Yet they have a profound effect on a student's performance in school.

I'm not passing judgment. Everyone's busier than they'd like to be. I'm simply saying that when you're looking at why a student isn't performing in school make sure you look at the whole picture.

Putting the "Fun" in Fundraising

Forget about selling candy bars. School fundraisers today are big business.

I can't help but wonder what message we send to kids when they observe some of the wacky ways we raise money to pay for their education. Adults repeatedly tell them that a good education is the key to a successful future. Yet we don't always put our money where our mouth is. As a result, kids see us scramble to come up with money to fund the very education that we insist is so vital to their future.

It's criminal that fundraising is even necessary in one of the richest, most powerful countries in the world. Yet it's a testament to our determination and resourcefulness that we do it.

Long gone are the days of bake sales, book fairs, and dunk tanks, though. These days PTAs are more in need of a CEO than energetic moms.

In Nevada, lawmakers proposed a tax on brothels to pay for education. In Seattle, the Economic Opportunity Institute initiated a campaign to tax espresso to pay for education. In Berkeley, California, parents took to the streets to convince city residents to donate their $400 rebate checks from the federal government. Rapper P. Diddy vowed to raise $1 million for New York City schools by running the New York City Marathon, and challenged Oprah Winfrey to match that amount.

Parents in several districts have even created private educational foundations to cultivate public–private partnerships, and silent auctions featuring high-end prizes might bring them $200,000 or more.

E-commerce sites are perhaps the most powerful trend, though. These sites allow users to choose the schools they'd like to help, then links them with big-name retailers such as Amazon.com. When users make a purchase at one of those sites, up to 20 percent of that purchase goes to their school of choice.

I thought I'd heard it all when it came to fundraising when the residents of Junction City, Oregon, sold blood plasma to raise money for their schools. That seemed a little above and beyond the call, to me. Residents there also auctioned off the rights to hunt for buffalo and antelope on their property.

But then, they really outdid themselves.

The men of the Long Tom Grange in Junction City added a whole new dimension to fundraising for schools. Following the example of the prim, middle-aged ladies from northern England who made a tasteful, fully nude calendar to raise money for leukemia, these guys launched "A Shameless Fundraising Project," posing nude with strategically placed props.

For $1/ you got a peek at twelve ordinary, yet charming (and very pale) guys, ages forty to seventy, wearing nothing but their hats and a grin, twinkling for the camera.

Junction City looks like a wholesome, sweet, quiet town, and the PG-rated calendar reflects that. The guys became celebrities of sorts, and raised even more money by hosting calendar signings. It's the kind of slick PR move that you'd expect to see in a more cosmopolitan city, yet my guess is that they raised much more than the $25,000 they were hoping for.

Though there have been many spin-offs since the English ladies bared all, the men of Long Tom Grange think this is the first time it's been done to benefit education.

Intriguing, isn't it? What community member might you like to see posing on a calendar to raise money for our schools?

I hope that children don't assume that education is a low priority when they hear about budget shortfalls. I hope that they don't assume that education is a low priority when they see the adults around them scramble to raise funds.

I hope that the message they get is that education is so important that the adults in their lives will go to any lengths to pay for it.

Even if it means taking off their clothes.

Prom Paparazzi Teaches Entitlement

It was spring of 1976. My mom snapped one last picture as my date and I pulled away from the curb in his mother's wood-paneled Vista Cruiser station wagon. And happily, that was the last I saw of my parents on prom night. Back then, prom was a chance to dress up, go off into the night on our own, and act like grown-ups. At the dance, real grown-ups—our teachers—watched unobtrusively from the shadows and talked quietly among themselves, stifling yawns.

My, how things have changed.

High school proms have reached epic proportions, as kids try to outdo each other on a small-time version of the Hollywood red carpet. But on a night that is supposed to be a teen's debut into the world of adults, many parents can't seem to strike the right balance between hovering, and looking the other way.

I chaperoned my first prom in 1981 and over the years I observed firsthand a weird evolution in parental involvement. Because the arrival is everything, many folks get there before the kids and line both sides of the entrance, a parental paparazzi lying in wait. Bedazzled kids step from limos into flashing strobes and whirring camcorders as parents strain to capture every precious second of the long red carpet walk.

You'd think parents would pack up and go home then, but they don't. The parental unit—sometimes dragging along younger brothers and sisters—follow the kids into the prom, recording everything from the buffet line to the prom picture line. Like some bizarre reality show, nothing is too trivial to capture on film.

Ironically, and perhaps by tacit agreement with their children, they often leave just when they should stay, and miss what they need to see—teachers repeatedly reminding students that their dancing is too dirty, and if they don't stop they'll have to leave. Those parental shutterbugs certainly don't venture to the after-prom festivities in the rented hotel room, either. What Kodak moments are they missing there?

The look-at-me generation seems to equate a good time with the size of the spectacle. But it's just a school dance, not a coronation. For the kids' part, I don't see how prom can possibly live up to the hype and expense that currently surrounds it. Do they actually have any fun? Do they know how to have fun without being the center of attention? Isn't all that peer pressure terribly stressful?

I've observed the parent–child relationship of hundreds of students. And if you think your only job as a parent is to be your child's biggest fan, then you've taught a fine lesson in narcissism and entitlement.

But how on earth will your child cope when the rest of the world doesn't find them quite so fascinating?

I'll Have a Popcorn, a Diploma, and a Large Coke, Please

Be careful what you wish for.

That's what I say to parents who complain that they aren't given enough tickets to their child's graduation ceremony, or that the school auditorium is too small. Because believe me, this trend of holding the graduation ceremony in a large sports arena makes the event lose its pomp.

Being jammed into a small auditorium has some advantages. For one thing, there's a certain amount of accountability if you're sitting close to someone who wants to hear the speeches. If you make too much noise they're bound to shush you, or at least give you the evil eye. For another thing, no one gets up and moves around because there's nowhere to go.

Not so for graduations held in sports arenas.

In a circus-like atmosphere complete with a hot almond stand, concessions, air horns, and cowbells, many guests come simply to socialize. They wander in late, talk, laugh, and look for friends. After sitting in one spot for a while, they move on. They come to see and be seen, and anything happening on the dais takes second stage to that.

That's the problem with graduation in an arena: *too many* people can attend. I've been to seven sports arena graduations and the behavior of the audience just keeps getting worse.

From the principal's opening remarks to the last hurrah, few in the audience pay attention. Kids run free, cell phones chirp, and people wearing jeans and tennis shoes climb up and down the stairs balancing huge buckets of popcorn and jumbo Cokes. Even the broom-crew is out in force, constantly sweeping up after the litterbugs.

The crowd starts out restless and gets worse. Apparently no one can go two hours without a snack, and the length of the line at the concession stand grows in direct proportion to the length of the speeches.

Constant chatter and movement make it hard to pay attention, but some try. On either side of the dais, closest to the graduates, parents and family listen intently. They arrived early enough to get what passes for a good seat in this gigantic warehouse. Their hands hold cameras, rather than nachos or hot pretzels. Unfortunately, they're still too far away to get a decent photo of their child unless they have a telephoto lens, but they try. This small core of people is engaged in the ceremony. The rest of the crowd is superfluous.

The worst offenders are other teenagers. It would be nice to think they were there for inspiration, to contemplate their own graduation. But, no. Groups of teenagers wearing baseball caps, sunglasses perched on top, skulk around with cell phones glued to their ears. They ignore the speakers until they hear applause, chime in with a guttural, "*Yeah!*" and promptly go back to their conversations. And because it's such a big place, they're anonymous. There's no one to tell them to behave.

Don't get me wrong, school officials work hard to put on a well-orchestrated, dignified ceremony, in spite of the setting and some of the guests. But let's face it, if you hold a ceremony in a sports arena, people behave like they're at a sporting event. All sense of decorum is lost. Any family looking for an intimate experience is going to be sadly disappointed.

Schools move their graduations to sports arenas because the size of stepfamilies and extended families mean most high school gymnasiums and auditoriums are too small. Like many innovations, moving graduation to an arena probably seemed like a good idea at the time. But we're either going to have to adjust to graduation under the big top, or we're going to have to move it back to the school and limit the tickets.

Forget about pomp and circumstance.

In an arena it's just chomp and circulate.

CHAPTER 8

Public Schools

THE EVER-EVOLVING
AMERICAN INSTITUTION

Rigor and Relevance Mean
Squat without the Relationship

Rigor, relevance, relationships.

Hot buzzwords right now, this is the magic combination that will purportedly transform education as we know it.

The theory behind this latest educational trend is that if we raise the level of our expectations and make the work rigorous, choose educational experiences that are relevant, and concentrate on creating good relationships, all children will learn.

It's got a good ring to it, too, which is why it's been bandied about so much and is being hailed as the new three Rs of learning.

But the dirty truth is that rigor has squeezed out both relevance and relationships.

All over the country states are mandating more rigorous high school curricula. Yet the new requirements so completely fill a student's schedule that it leaves little room for electives—which are often of most relevance to students.

Teaching to the almighty standardized test is rigorous, too, though it's questionable whether those tests are relevant.

Students tell us that much of what they're forced to study is irrelevant. That doesn't mean that it is, just that they perceive it that way. Students repeatedly told me that they wanted hands-on lessons, learning that is immediately useful.

But creating more meaningful relationships in education? We're doing nothing more than paying lip service to that. In today's test-driven, data-dominated, documentation-crazed, super-consolidated world of education, the relationship is the first thing to go. We're so busy processing students that we lose sight of the real live human beings behind the numbers and stats.

A high school teacher with thirty kids in one fifty-five-minute class has a scant minute and a half a day to spend with each student—if they have nothing else to do. But there's a lot to do. Working through a five-pound textbook in 180 days leaves little time for less pressing things, like getting to know each other.

Guiding and nurturing young people into becoming productive adults, and the joy of connecting with kids, is why teachers teach. And students crave teachers who take the time to care about them as a person and recognize their individuality.

But adding rigor for the student adds it for the teacher, too, which would be fine if it didn't squeeze out relationship-building time with kids.

Experts point to that disconnect—that lack of relationships with positive adult role models—as one reason for so much school violence.

Here's the thing that noneducators just don't get: the relationship is the key to both rigor and relevance. A student will work hard for a teacher that "gets" them, a teacher they like and respect. And they'll really listen when that teacher explains the relevance of what they're doing.

Rigor? Bring it on.

Relevance? Absolutely.

But without a relationship to build on? It's just more educational rhetoric.

Doing Themselves In

It won't be test scores, unqualified teachers, or the corporate agenda that will ultimately result in the demise of the public school system.

Nope. Lack of fortitude is what will do it in.

Ask veteran teachers how administration has changed over the years, and they will tell you that their biggest gripe is that administrators don't back teachers. In the old days, if a teacher sent a student to the office, almost without exception a principal would discipline that child, no questions asked.

For better or worse though, those days are gone. Now, if a teacher sends a student to the office, the teacher is questioned about the incident as exhaustively as the kid. "Are you sure this is what you saw? What you heard? How it started?" Teachers tell me that this questioning even happens in front of students, further undermining their authority.

Granted, administrators are busier than ever, and understandably resent handling discipline that a teacher should handle. It's a valid complaint—some teachers are too quick to send a child to the office rather than cultivate their own discipline strategies.

Gone too are the days of "If you get in trouble at school you'll get in more trouble at home." Now kids in trouble say, "Get my mom on the phone. She'll straighten this out." Parents are the true power players in the public school equation. And therein lies the problem.

In our litigious society, parents are quick to threaten lawsuits, most of which are ridiculous. Yet administrators too often react reflexively, protectively, going to great lengths to keep the customer satisfied. And know this—the customer is not the student—it's the parent.

Keeping parents happy is a matter of survival. An unhappy parent now has options and may just take their child elsewhere. And in state funding, students equal money.

Let's say a student steals a cell phone and gets caught. Parents argue that as long as he gives it back, he should go unpunished. Administrators go along to keep the parent happy—and make the problem disappear. But it's exactly that kind of slow undermining of discipline that creates an undisciplined student body. And disenfranchised teachers.

So this mission to keep the customer satisfied has dangerous side effects. It compromises discipline policies. And compromised discipline policies mean a compromised learning environment. Parents who want more—not an undisciplined student body, a weak learning environment, and disenfranchised teachers—will seek alternative schools anyway.

Inadvertently then, unconsciously, with the best of intentions, by trying to save themselves, the school system is slowly doing itself in.

Public schools are under incredible scrutiny right now. This is not the time to relax standards for behavior. Now is the time for school boards and administrators to stand up to politicians, lawyers, and the loud minority of threatening parents.

This is the time for courage, not compromise.

Reading, Writing, and Retainers

"We have nothing to fear but fear itself," according to Franklin Roosevelt.

Obviously Frank has never worked in a public school system in this day and age, because we have a lot to be afraid of.

Namely, lawsuits.

Which is why I loved the television drama *Boston Public*. It was one of the most realistic television shows about the public school system for one simple reason: It accurately portrayed the nuttiness of working in a high school. It poignantly captured that slightly out-of-control feeling that big high schools have, that sense that just when you think you've *really* heard it all, something comes along that tops it.

The most believable aspect of the show was the administrators' almost manic fear of lawsuits. Every thought, every decision, every move they made was run through their mental lawsuit-o-meter, which tried to determine how the decision would stand up in court.

The lawsuit-o-meter is second only to the press-o-meter, which tried to determine how the decision would look if it ended up splashed across the front page of a newspaper.

All school personnel fear lawsuits. We constantly second-guess ourselves, and the big and small decisions we make.

"Okay, Johnny, that's the fifth time I've caught you writing on your desk. I'll see you at lunch and you can clean all of the desks in the room."

But wait.

Will this scar Johnny for life? Will he grow up to have a cleaning phobia and come back ten years from now and sue me? Will he turn into a child abuser, making his own children clean and clean and clean?

Is this humiliating to him? Will the other kids tease him for this, and if they do, will he lash out violently and perhaps get a gun and shoot us all?

What if he develops a rash from the cleaning spray? What if he gets a headache from the smell? What if he develops cleaning elbow and it ruins his potential for a career in professional sports?!

Is it worth the risk, or should I just clean this desk myself (again)?

So here is my prediction: in the very near future every school will have a lawyer on staff. I don't mean that each school district will have a lawyer on retainer, as they currently do. I mean they will hire a full-time lawyer for every building in the district, with an office right next to the principal's.

Teachers will have the lawyer's number on speed dial on their classroom phones and every time they have a question they'll dial him up.

"Uh, Mr. Lawyer, my students are doing a social studies project that requires them to trace their family trees . . ."

"No, Mr. Teacher, you can't require them to do that, because kids who have unsavory characters in their lineage may be embarrassed."

Or, "Ms. Lawyer, I think I'm in trouble. I put Johnny's A+ essay on the bulletin board and now his mother is angry because the kids are calling him a nerd."

"You're right, Mrs. Teacher, you are in trouble. You need to take measures to fix this immediately. Write a letter of apology to Johnny and his mother. Maybe we can nip this one in the bud."

You laugh, but these examples are real.

Fear-based decisions are not good decisions, but lawsuits are costly, time-consuming, and they bring negative press, three things school districts can't afford.

And the best offense is a good defense, right?

Grade Inflation Tarnishes those Shiny As

There's a dirty little secret that school administrators don't want you to know. Grade inflation is alive and well, even in your school.

Education has gone the way of dentists and ambulance chasers, and schools are practically advertising on street corners to lure clients. It's a competitive business and some schools play the game better than others, using slick videos and colorful brochures to tout the finer qualities of their school. And in the eyes of John and Jane Q. Public, a school where most of the students get good grades must be a better school.

Student grade point averages are rising, but ACT and SAT scores are not. So what's the deal? Do the A students experience a brain melt the day of the test and do poorly?

No. It's called grade inflation and it's basically the slow erosion of educational requirements and standards. It's giving a student an A for B work, or passing them with a D– when they have actually failed. It's a teacher requiring less for an A than they did five years ago.

Administrators don't come right out and tell teachers to lower standards to raise grades. But they don't tell them to raise standards, either. Administrators tell teachers to improve student learning.

Well, pardon me, but, *duh*. Teachers would dance the cha-cha or eat a fly if they thought it would help their students learn. That's why teachers use their own time and their own money to attend conferences, workshops, seminars, and classes, looking for that magic elixir that will ignite a spark of interest in the video-game-glazed eyes of their students.

Most of the teachers I know would rather clean the school cafeteria on fish stick Friday than give a student a grade he doesn't deserve. But the pressure from administrators and parents takes its toll.

When students get to high school where the work is decidedly more difficult, and grade point averages count for college admissions, suddenly an A student may struggle to get a B. The stunned parents pressure the teacher by telling the principal (and anyone else who will listen) that Johnny isn't a B student, he's never gotten Bs, there must be something wrong with these teachers if they can't see that *Johnny is an A student*!

It's as if the sheer force of their will can make it so. And often it does.

There are countless ways that teachers are pressured to inflate grades. Once early in my career, when I was a young and impressionable teacher, I complained to an assistant principal that my students weren't doing their homework. Her response was, "Then maybe you shouldn't give homework."

Most administrators are more subtle, though. The message may come through an administrator who pleads the case of an ineligible athlete before a big game.

The message may come through an administrator who calls you into his office to have a little chat about the number of students who have earned Fs in your class. Worse yet, some schools tie teacher evaluations to student performance. If you want a real recipe for disaster, that's it.

Teachers are not blameless when it comes to grade inflation. Nobody likes to see hard work go unrewarded, especially in an environment where laziness abounds, so sometimes a teacher might raise a student's grade a bit for extra effort. And kids and administrators alike know which teachers in a school are the "easy" teachers and which ones are tough.

The bottom line is this: now that schools are competing for clients, fair and accurate student assessment often falls victim to the money game.

Your student's A may not be the same A you earned in high school.

Grading Agony

"My God, wasn't that painful to watch?" my husband, a former teacher, asked as the final credits rolled for the movie *The Emperor's Club*. I didn't have to ask what he meant—I knew. He was referring to the agonizing, distressing decisions that teachers make every day.

In the movie Mr. Hundert, a teacher at a prestigious old school for boys, struggles to reach one rebellious student, Sedgewick Bell, the neglected son of an unscrupulous senator. Eventually he connects with the boy. When Bell finishes one point away from the finals in the Julius Caeser contest, an important academic competition, Mr. Hundert gives him the point, hoping to fan the flames of Bell's intellectual curiosity.

Of course it ends badly. Bell cheats during the competition, Mr. Hundert calls him on it, and Bell unashamedly admits it. The fragile bond is broken, and Bell returns to his bad boy ways.

It's a variation on a story that's played out repeatedly in schools every where. Trust me when I tell you that teachers spend hours agonizing over student grades.

Let's say a student's point total falls just short of passing, at 59 percent. The teacher ponders the big picture: How many assignments were (or were not) turned in? How was class participation? Tardiness? Attendance? Were there extenuating circumstances, like a death in the family, or illness?

Most important, though, what is this student's attitude toward learning? Did she try, or did she slough off until the last minute panic? Because that's what matters most to a teacher—that a student be willing to try. Rules will be bent and accommodations will be made for a student who tries.

But it's never an easy decision. We gaze into our crystal ball to see what the student might learn from this favor. Will he see it as a gift, an opportunity to get his act together and do better? Or will he see it as a way of working the system, a means to an end? Will he think he's the exception to the rule all his life? Would it be better in the long run to let him feel the consequences of his actions? And in giving one student a break, are we ultimately being unfair to another student?

If it works, and the student learns from the incident, we feel buoyant, optimistic, vindicated. But when it doesn't, and a student continues a downhill spiral, we feel duped, sad, and profoundly disappointed, in the student and inexplicably, in ourselves. It's a personal struggle, one of many that teachers face.

Ultimately Bell just works the system. Several years later, a successful Bell invites Mr. Hundert to facilitate a rematch of the Julius Caesar contest, and he cheats again.

As Mr. Hundert said, "However much we stumble, it is a teacher's burden always to hope, that with learning, a boy's character might be changed, and so the destiny of a man."

Teachers, regardless of the burden, never cease to hope.

The High Price of Teaching

We're all guilty of it. You've done it, and so have I. We've all scoffed in envy at the salary, vacation, or perks of one profession or another.

For me, it's professional athletes. I can't fathom why they earn such exorbitant salaries just because they can throw a fastball or slam dunk a basketball.

Ah, but teacher pay, now there's kindling for a firestorm of debate.

When I taught there were days when I had so much fun I couldn't believe I got paid to do it. And then there were days when I left that building thinking there wasn't enough money in the world to make me go back.

Once while sitting in a doctor's waiting room I saw a young woman intently grading papers while she waited. As I watched I remembered the psychological weight of that pile of papers that never got smaller because there was always a new assignment. And if you got behind, that pile had the potential to get so big so fast that you had fantasies of it accidentally catching on fire and turning to ash.

I'll bet that teacher graded a few papers here and there all evening, squeezing in a few while the pasta was boiling, or during TV commercials.

One teacher told me this at the end of first marking period: "In total (all classes) I have graded 4,872 assignments so far this year. Average grading time is five minutes (twenty minutes for essays to less than a minute for easy stuff). I have spent a total of seventeen days [outside of school] grading!"

Another teacher complained to me about the high cost of teacher certification. After earning her bachelor's degree and paying tuition to student teach for a semester, unpaid, she paid for fingerprinting and a background check by the FBI, a basic skills test, tests in her major and minor, and her provisional certificate, which is good for six years.

Once she lands a job, she must complete fifteen days of professional development (beyond what the district requires) in the first three years, at her own expense. Then she must acquire eighteen credit hours (at $350 to $475 per credit hour) to get her professional certificate, and pay for both requirements. Then she must take six credits every five years at her own expense, for the rest of her career. Add to that, books, gas for out-of-town classes, and parking. It costs a lot to be a teacher.

Some believe that if teachers were paid less there could be more money spent on students. But look at southern states where teachers are poorly paid—they still have old, out-of-date buildings and the same budget problems all schools face.

If you've decided that teachers are overpaid and underworked, I can't change your mind. But consider this: twenty percent of all new teachers leave within three years. In urban districts, 50 percent leave within five years.

So if it's really such a cake job, why aren't people waiting in line to be hired?

The Peter Principle, Alive and Well

The ladder is narrow and short for people looking to move up in education. There aren't many top jobs in each district, and there are only about three rungs above the position of teacher.

So if the goal is to make a lot of money by becoming an education leader, you've got to job-hop. If a superintendent stays in one district the pay increases will be relatively small. But a move to a different, preferably larger district can bring big money. And that's okay. Everyone has the right to pursue the highest salary that he or she can. But it means that superintendent turnover is huge—and everyone seems to know it except the school boards that do the hiring. They continue to hire outsiders, believing that they'll stay forever, while ignoring excellent candidates right under their own noses.

When a superintendent hops from district to district, never staying longer than two years, his ability is as illusory as the wizard's. He sells a flashy idea, but never has to prove that it works. As soon as he leaves another superintendent comes along selling a different flashy idea, creating a different illusion. A superintendent who knows he is not going to stay can say absolutely anything he wants about what he knows and can do. He will be long gone before he has to prove it.

Ultimately, the people who are left behind—the students, parents, educators, and community—pay the price. They're left with low morale, canceled programs, and an undone to-do list.

A wise school board chooses someone with strong roots in her own community, someone who will have to answer to friends and family, someone who understands the district's history, culture, and traditions. Someone who will stay around to see if the changes work.

To make matters worse, school boards pay big bucks for a superintendent search by a company that knows nothing about the district, its clientele, and its needs.

Many years ago, my school district hired one of those companies that specialize in superintendent searches. The district paid them thousands of public tax dollars to find a "perfect fit."

Representatives from the company set up shop in the teachers' lounge for a few days chatting with staff and passing out surveys. The whole concept seemed silly to me; why pay a group of strangers big money to do something we could do? Isn't that what our human resource department was for? How could they possibly know us better than we knew ourselves?

I pondered this as I sat in the lounge, munching my sandwich, listening to the friendly lady question my colleagues. Finally, I piped up.

"What, exactly, do you do for the $10,000 our district is paying you?" I asked. The nice lady said they survey the staff and community to find out what they want in a superintendent, and then find candidates who match that description.

"Well, where do you find them?" I asked.

From education journals and websites, the smiling lady said.

"Well, what, exactly, do you do that we couldn't do ourselves?" I asked. "I mean, we can survey our own staff and community. We can find candidates in journals and on websites."

Apparently, I went too far because the smiling lady stopped smiling. But I couldn't stop.

"It just seems like a lot of money to pay for something we could have done ourselves," I persisted.

She packed up in a huff and marched off to the other lounge.

I thought about that conversation a lot over the next few years as I watched the superintendent they chose alienate staff, dismantle our school culture and traditions, promote top-down management over site-based decision making, destroy staff morale, and basically tick off just about everyone she came in contact with.

I don't know if she grew as tired of us as we did of her, if she was forced out, or if it was just time for a career move, but eventually, she started looking elsewhere.

And guess what?

Soon there was another interview team in our lounge, this time asking us all kinds of questions about our superintendent's performance.

What a dilemma. If we told the truth we could be stuck with her forever. But if we were crafty, we just might be rid of her. This may be our only chance! What to do, *what to do*?

Well. We did the only thing we could do.

We gave her a glowing report.

Merit Pay Won't Fix Education

Almost every teaching staff has a slacker. Mine did. Consummate lounge lizard, he had a student keep attendance, never gave homework, and his lesson plan consisted of a workbook. I have no idea what his evaluations looked like, but based on the amount of time he spent kissing up, I'll bet they were fine.

I, on the other hand, worked my behind off. And it ticked me off royally to see him spend hours drinking coffee and chatting up the secretaries while I slogged through another stack of student essays, or came in at 6 a.m. to set up for a big project.

Ninety-nine percent of my colleagues were hard working, dedicated people who performed small miracles every day. But there's waste in every profession: careless doctors, incompetent lawyers, dishonest CEOs, lazy line workers.

Still, I can only roll my eyes heavenward at the nationwide push to tie teacher pay to merit and performance.

Merit pay? If my pay had been based on how I stacked up next to the slacker, I would have been in like Flynn.

But if my pay had been based on the test scores of my students? Some years I would have been eating steak and lobster because the learning happened so effortlessly. But the year I taught Reading and Writing Lab it would have been nothing but weenies and beans. My nineteen special education students made every lesson a battle of wills.

Noneducators think teachers should be held more accountable. Good teachers agree. Most would love to be recognized for good attendance, innovative lesson plans, committee involvement, professional development, ability to work with staff and community. But they don't want to be held accountable for things that are out of their control, like student attendance, low IQs, poor parenting, and yes, low test scores. Too many variables contribute to those scores.

And consider this: Countless teachers make huge impacts in troubled students' lives, even if they aren't able to raise their test scores. Does that have less merit?

And you think grades are inflated now? Just wait. Teachers are pressured every day by parents and administrators to raise grades. Imagine if their salary depended on it, too.

Perhaps the biggest problem is who's going to decide? The school board? That's scary. Administrators? If that were the case, the suck-up on my staff would be rich.

As a solution to what ails education, merit pay for teachers is shortsighted and narrow. The problems are rooted in society, not the teaching staff.

Still, merit pay is worth looking into. And since it's their bright idea, I suggest we start with politicians. No perks, no pay raises until they prove their worth.

Wait—what? That's not fair, you say? We can't hold politicians accountable for the woes of the constituents they represent?

Really.

What, Exactly, Are We Selling?

Early in my teaching career I used to look around at all of the great things my colleagues were doing in their classrooms and think, "Gee, too bad we don't advertise. We really need to figure out a way to get the word out about all of the cool things we're doing around here."

But now that school districts are spending big bucks to advertise, I'm not so sure it's a good idea.

In the marketing wars between charter, parochial, and public schools, will the winners be the students? Will the competition create an improvement in services for children? If so, then I say let's don the gloves and jump into the ring.

But what if it doesn't? What if it turns into a competition to see who can raise the most money, hire the best marketers, and create the slickest ad campaign? Are we diverting time, money, and energy away from the task at hand, which is teaching and learning?

Public schools typically function in reactive rather than proactive mode and most school districts' marketing campaigns are no exception. Often their goal is not to solicit new clients, but to mercly hold onto the students they expect to lose each year.

Public schools have a long history of scrambling to keep up in an ever-changing society. Now school officials have the added task of creating budgets that accommodate advertising on billboards and taking out radio ads.

And after all, how can you tell if a school system is good? Can a shiny brochure truly tell the whole story?

Can it tell a lie?

Until fairly recently, kids simply attended the school district where they lived. But having more schools to choose from has parents examining more intangible things like grade point averages, which can be, and often are, inflated.

How about test scores? The government, which has deep pockets when it needs them, has spent big bucks to convince John Q. Public that test scores tell the whole story about a school. But they don't.

Teacher certification? It depends. A teaching certificate doesn't necessarily make a good teacher. It does, however, ensure a well-rounded education and exposure to a variety of teaching strategies and subject mastery.

Discipline statistics? Now that would be telling. You can learn a lot about a school district by the kinds of discipline problems it has and how it handles them. School districts that have a firm hand on discipline usually have an effective learning environment. If classrooms are orderly, learning is more likely. But that's something you won't see in a brochure. School districts guard their discipline statistics like a woman guards her weight.

As with most services, the best way to choose a school system is by reputation and word of mouth. Ask around. How strong are the discipline policies? Is the general consensus that district officials uphold them consistently? How do they handle the tough, politically charged issues like student organizations for atheists, or the Day of Silence for gays? How often and how well do they communicate with parents?

Some districts simply have better internal PR systems and are just more guarded, more careful to let the good news out and keep the bad news in.

Good PR is more than a slick radio ad. Good PR is years of good work that builds on itself. All of the slick ad campaigns in the world won't work if there's nothing to back them up. People are too smart for that.

When all is said and done, we would be better off if school districts spent that money, time, and energy to improve their services. The rest will fall into place.

In the meantime, consumers beware: ads that sound too good to be true probably are.

Tests great, less failing?

Oh, I can see it all now.

The Cheesewagon Blues

Tough jobs abound in the public school system.

Principals, for example, spend more time than they'd like disciplining kids. Teaching, of course, is fraught with its own bittersweet aggravations. Custodians dread the flu season and those "cleanup on aisle four" calls. And the sweet cafeteria ladies who manage to feed hundreds of kids in a mere half hour suffer nothing but complaints no matter what they serve.

Every player is key on the public school team. But none so literally holds the life of each and every child in his hands, as the school bus driver.

On difficult days when my freshmen seemed to bounce off the walls, I'd sigh with guilty relief when the buses arrived. Watching kids race outside I'd think—oh, those poor bus drivers! What nerves of steel they must have to drive a bus full of rambunctious kids.

And sometimes after school a tense voice would come through the main office walkie-talkie: "This is bus number 24. I'm bringing 'em back. Send a principal to meet me in the parking lot." Off the principal would hustle to meet the bus and restore order.

It also wasn't unusual to walk through the office before school even started and see a line of students outside the principal's office, waiting to be disciplined for misbehaving on the bus on the ride in.

So I was excited when I got to spend the afternoon with a group of bus drivers in their lounge, and hear the tales of the road. And I learned that, yes, maintaining order while you're piloting a huge vehicle takes composure.

Elementary kids, they told me, are the noisiest. Junior high kids, the most difficult. High school kids, the most intimidating. Problems on board run the gamut from writing on seats or eating and drinking, to disrespectful language, urinating, fighting, smoking, or inappropriate displays of affection.

The consensus among drivers, though, is that if you're good with kids, discipline isn't an issue. Kids usually respond well to fair and firm direction. And if safety is at stake, drivers do have the option of requesting that a principal revoke a student's riding privilege.

If you dread driving to work in the first snow of the year, school bus drivers feel that tenfold. Road construction is another headache, especially since time is the enemy as they strive to reach each stop on time.

Every driver I talked to agreed that though those things make the job challenging, it's not the biggest complaint. Nor is it the biggest threat to the safety of your children.

The biggest threat is the other drivers on the road.

Though it seems you couldn't miss a 16,000 pound, thirty-five-foot-long, bright yellow school bus with eight flashing red lights, every driver told me that four to five times a day cars ignore those lights and blow right past. Often, they're talking on a cell phone.

Each October schools across the country celebrate National School Bus Safety Week. But the observance is, of course, just a formality.

Those flashing yellow and red lights are important every day of the year.

The Building Speaks . . .

My name is John F. Kennedy High School. I am a public school, an institution of learning, paid for and owned by the people in my community. I was built in 1965 in a rural suburb of an industrial blue-collar city.

Thousands of students have passed through my halls. Some have gone on to do great things, to become doctors and artists and humanitarians. Some, I'm sad to say, have not done well. A few have landed in prison.

To many, I am just a building, cold brick and steel, drab institutional colors adorning my walls. But I am more than just a building. I am the heart of the community, opening my doors to one and all. When school is not in session, college classes, enrichment classes, elections, even craft fairs are held here. I don't discriminate on religion, color, or creed, though sometimes the people inside of me do.

I've seen many changes since my doors opened in 1965. I watched as typewriters were carried out and computers carried in. I saw 8 mm projectors first replaced with TVs and VCRs, and then DVD players. I saw slide rules replaced with calculators.

My biggest challenge now (and also for my people) is to keep up with technology. My wiring is old and not equipped to take the strain of hundreds of computers, printers, scanners, televisions, and fax machines. Gang plugs and outlet strips have been added everywhere, but still, sometimes it's just too much and I blow a fuse.

In the 1970s my glass windows were replaced with energy efficient panels, making my classrooms and hallways dark. In the 1980s my terrazzo floors were covered with carpet in an effort to soundproof my rooms. In the 1990s the carpet was taken back out because some of my students had allergies to mold and dust trapped in that carpet.

My large, spacious classrooms have been divided into smaller classrooms to accommodate special education classes. My metal shop has been replaced with a modern technology lab. My charming old-fashioned chalkboards have been replaced with white dry-erase boards and smelly erasable markers.

My cafeteria has gone from serving real meals on real plates with real utensils, to serving fast food on Styrofoam plates with plastic utensils. No one makes kids clean up after themselves anymore, however, and after lunch my floors are littered with candy wrappers and food, my tables covered with abandoned milk cartons and water bottles. Amid much controversy, pop machines were installed in the 1980s only to be taken back out this year.

For the most part, I am well cared for. My custodians sweep my floors and tend to my ailments, but my students seem to be increasingly careless. They stuff paper towels into my toilets for the pleasure of watching them run over, and empty my soap dispensers onto the floor. Gum and graffiti are everywhere.

So many fads have come and gone. Long, unwashed hippie hair, afros, mall bangs, mullets. My floors have been traversed by everything from canvas Converse tennis shoes, to ridiculously expensive shoes that light up, to shoes that work like roller skates, with little wheels built in. Platform shoes and bellbottoms went out of style and came back again. I even remember when female teachers were not allowed to wear pants.

I have felt the trepidation of the freshmen's first day and the exuberance of the seniors' last. Love, hate, anger, jealousy, joy, grief, sorrow. I am witness to all of the drama that unfolds here day after day, as children make the transition from adolescence to adulthood.

The students, the support staff, the principals, the teachers. I love and embrace them all.

If my walls could talk, oh, the stories they would tell. . . .

. . . About the Kids

Thousands of students have come through my doors since I opened in 1965, and though their clothing and hairstyles have changed, their hopes and fears have not.

Omniscience has granted me the power to see into the hearts and minds of all who walk my halls. If only they could see each other as clearly as I see them.

Rick is one of my more troubled students. He has endured many labels during his time in the public school system. Slow learner. Misfit. Loner. Degenerate.

Rick's stepfather smacked his mother, hard, right across the mouth before he left for school this morning. Rick hates his stepfather, with a hatred so deep it makes his gut ache. He wanted to step in, to beat the crap out of the guy, but his mother, blood oozing from the corner of her mouth, just screamed at him to get out, to go to school.

He hates school, but he hates home, too. Anyway, there was nothing he could do if he stayed. The creep and his mother were still half crocked from the night before, and would pass out soon, only to wake up in time to drink their dinner again.

He's angry with his mother for staying with the creep, ashamed to come from where he does. He's angry, too, at his real dad for leaving when Rick was only three. His face is dark with anger as he steps off the bus, roughly pushing a puny freshman out of the way. He ducks into the bathroom and lights up, then takes out his pocketknife and carves a deep gash into the freshly painted stall door, picturing the creep's face.

Tessa has her own problems. Bookish and brilliant, she has wanted to be a surgeon ever since her parents told her she did when she was six years old. She gets off the bus and heads straight for the library, eager to do some research before the first bell.

The other kids call her Teachers' Pet, and the teachers do love her, simply because she makes their job so easy. Learning is effortless for her, and the other kids make her pay for this. She, too, has endured many labels, labels given to her by other students. Nerd. Braniac. Four-eyes. Einstein. The name-calling hurts, but she pretends that it doesn't.

Tessa is stressed. Her parents are both surgeons and they expect her to be making the dean's list at Harvard in exactly two years. When she thinks about the possibility of not getting in her stomach cramps and her heart races.

Some of my students simply get lost in the crowd. Brooke feels insignificant, like an outsider. Timid and wary, she shuffles through the halls with her head down, disappointed that no one notices her, but terrified that they might.

She is an average looking girl who gets average grades. She doesn't cause trouble and she is often overlooked or ignored. Her fifth hour teacher still doesn't know her name.

Brooke is rarely absent, never tardy, and has never been sent to the office. She doesn't play sports, is not in any clubs, and doesn't have any close friends. Boys look right through her and she knows it. No one has bothered to label her anything.

If only my students and teachers could know each other as well as I know them. They would be kinder to each other, the rites of adolescence would be easier, and high school wouldn't seem like such a mean, cold place.

. . . About the Staff

The unsung heroes here are the support staff. And they are aptly named. They support, in dozens of ways, the teaching and learning that happens here.

Custodians, secretaries, cooks, bus drivers, teachers' assistants. I could not function without them.

But the role of my custodians is misunderstood. My students think that my custodians are here for the sole purpose of cleaning up after them, when in fact they are here to look after *me*, to repair my windows, change my lightbulbs and wax my floors. My custodians are not here to clean up after overindulged children.

It's regrettable. Their job is unnecessarily nauseating. It's true that in addition to building maintenance, they must clean up vomit and blood spills, and unclog toilets.

But the sheer piggyness of kids can be stupefying. Are there no manners anymore? No sense of decorum at all? I wonder, sometimes, what their homes look like. Surely they are required to pick up after themselves there. Do high school kids play in their food at home? Do they walk through the living room dropping candy wrappers as they go?

I can feel Harry Schmidt's frustration. He shakes his head and sighs as he enters the cafeteria. Tray after tray left on the tables, in spite of the huge trash bins. For kicks, many kids pour the remains of their pop or milk into their leftover food, stirring it into a thick, smelly goo. The trays are almost overflowing and Harry has to pick them up carefully, lest the flimsy Styrofoam bends and the goo is spilled.

Is it a game to see who can make the biggest mess?

Ugh. It's enough to make him vomit. Some wise guy has stuffed a yellow condom full of peaches and stood it on end on the tray, then squeezed ketchup around it. Harry dumps it into the trash can and moves on, wishing for hidden surveillance cameras. Their parents should see this.

There's probably enough wasted food here to feed at least a hundred hungry kids every day. Harry wonders why they buy the food if they don't want it. Even the brown bag lunches, lovingly packed by someone at home, are largely wasted, smashed, and mutilated.

After school Harry sweeps the halls and classrooms in his wing. By the end of his route he has picked up twenty-three pens and pencils, twelve textbooks, six notebooks, and $2.36 worth of change.

A quiet, gentle soul, Harry is a churchgoing man, but he has ceased to be shocked at the filthy graffiti written on the desks. He has scrubbed the desks so many times in the sixteen years he's been here that the finish is coming off.

He moves on to the most dreaded job of the day. The student bathrooms. He goes into the boys', hoping there's nothing too awful today.

Luckily, it's not too bad. He flushes all of the toilets and urinals, wondering, again, if kids behave this way at home. Did no one teach them to flush a toilet after they use it? Using three different buckets and bleach, he cleans the toilets, sinks, and floor, then shuffles out.

When parents send their children off to school, they place their trust in many: the bus drivers, who get them here safely, the secretaries, who handle their paperwork, the cooks who feed them.

And the custodians. Always in the background, but always there, taking care of me.

And everyone else.

. . . About the Administrators

Of all of the public servants who walk my halls, perhaps the role of building principal has changed the most since I opened my doors in 1965.

Then, most principals across the state were middle-aged white men. The principal of an elementary school was often the only man in a building full of female teachers. Now, fortunately, there is more diversity.

A good principal is a gift, a visionary offering guidance to students and teachers alike. A bad principal is a drain on the morale and energy of everyone, allowing students and teachers to falter alone, without support or guidance.

In my early days, teachers worked their way up through the ranks to become principals in the district that they knew and loved. Now, principals are sought from other districts. Sometimes they bring with them a fresh approach and new ideas. But sometimes, in their zest to share these new ideas, they destroy the culture of a district they don't really understand.

The very first principal to lead my teaching and learning family was Mr. Maxheimer, an affable and well-liked varsity football coach and phys. ed. teacher with a master's degree in administration. Central admin. made it clear to him that a principal's job was his whenever he was ready. Membership in the good old boys club sealed the deal and ensured his success.

In those days, being a principal was a pretty nice job. His secretaries and teachers worked hard and made him look good. Sure, sometimes he put in long hours, but there was always time to kick back and talk sports with the coaches. By and large he was respected by parents and students alike, and when he made tough, unpopular decisions, he was (sometimes grudgingly) commended for his leadership.

Ms. O'Connell is the current principal of my building, but she had to work twice as hard as Maxheimer did to get here. There's no time for leisure in her day. She arrives early, stays late, and eats lunch at her desk. Because she's a woman, she is scrutinized more closely. When she makes tough, unpopular decisions, she's called a bitch.

School districts have not escaped the insanity of our litigious society. Looking back, Mr. Maxheimer can only remember being threatened with a lawsuit twice in his career. Ms. O'Connell is threatened with lawsuits almost daily.

Both principals wish they could spend less time disciplining kids. But even discipline has changed since the 1960s. Kids used to beg the principal not to call their parents when they were in trouble, hoping to be spared more trouble when they got home.

Now even kids in serious trouble strut into the office, discipline referral in hand, demanding, "Get my parents on the phone so they can come down here and straighten out this principal!"

Since Columbine, the responsibility of keeping her students safe weighs heavily on Ms. O'Connell. Safety issues take up more of her time, too, time that was already in short supply.

A principal's job used to be something to aspire to, a position of respect. But no more. Now it's a thankless job, one fewer and fewer people are willing to take.

I feel for the leaders of my teaching and learning family. The leadership of today's public school requires a very special person.

As Robert Gately said, "If leadership could be taught, all MBAs would be great leaders, and we know they are not."

. . . About the Teachers

I watch teachers trudge into my building day after day, arms laden with papers and books. Omniscience has granted me the power to see into their hearts and minds, see their concern for their students, their frustration, their exhaustion, their hope.

Miss Logan is in her second year of teaching. She has wanted to teach her whole life, and she believes that she can make a difference. Deeply spiritual, her first year was quite an eye-opener. The coarse language and disrespect from her students shocks and offends her. The shy, quiet kids are drawn to her gentle demeanor, sensing a safe place, but the tough kids sense fear, and like animals, they are quick to take advantage. She almost quit at the end of that first year, and still isn't sure if she'll stay. But this is her dream, and she's not ready to let it go. The reality of the job is just so very different from what she imagined that she almost can't believe it.

Mr. Luft went to college to avoid the draft in 1966. Star of his high school football team, he chose to teach so that he could coach. The jocks like him because with a little prodding he'll stray from the lesson and tell game stories all hour. Turns out, he's not all that crazy about teaching, but as his seniority grew it didn't seem prudent to leave. Now, he's lost his courage. What else could he do, anyway? He's got three kids in college and can't entertain the idea of starting over, so he tells himself that he loves his job, tells himself that he is good at it.

The youngest on the staff, Ms. Beck, is a top-notch teacher, engaging and enthusiastic. The kids like her because she's quick with a comeback, and doesn't take crap from any of them. But she feels that the sacrifices she makes to be here are just too great. Her friends, all bright and vibrant twentysomethings, are already making more money than she does, with a limitless potential for more. Their jobs have perks, too, bonuses and freebies and trips and panache. She works long, hard hours and doesn't have the time, energy, or money her friends have. It's sad. She won't be here long. The world is her oyster and as much as she likes the kids, there's just not enough incentive for her to stay.

Every school has many good, competent teachers. Most have only a sprinkling of exceptional teachers. Mrs. Garcia is an exceptional teacher. Mastery of subject, creativity, superior organizational skills, energy to burn, and charisma give her that certain something that even the most hardened kids can't resist. Just a little bit irreverent, she gets their attention and holds it. It helps that she doesn't have her own children and is able to spend all of her free time on schoolwork. Her lessons are so entertaining that kids leave her class amazed at how much they learned, amazed at how effortless it was.

You don't see what I see. Teachers here late at night, decorating their classrooms, working on lesson plans, grading papers. Tears privately shed over the sheer meanness of teenagers. Aching feet and aching backs and tired voices.

Our society has it all wrong; we pay professional athletes millions for playing a game, and our teachers a pittance for educating our future.

And still they teach.

Every day.

Our Most Important Mission

"Ms. Flynn, I just can't make up my mind. So, when I grow up I'm going to be a pediatrician, but I'll do hair at a salon in my spare time."

So said one of my eighth grade girls during a career project. She had a 1.5 grade point average and scored below average in reading comprehension. Most of the boys were certain—unequivocally—that they would become professional athletes—even the scrawny ones who played on no athletic team whatsoever.

I was always torn—should I burst their bubble and point them in a more realistic direction? Or should I play the consummate cheerleader and encourage them to follow their dreams no matter what?

I'm the first to say that public schools try to do too much. But one thing they don't do enough of is career education. Bullied by legislators who dictate the Priority-of-the-Year, too often schools have little time or money to spend on career exploration.

Yet, what is school if not a place to prepare for the future? If public schools don't do it, who will? Where else can kids learn about career options? Television? They'll end up thinking that being a lawyer is like *LA Law*—all courtroom drama, but no paperwork.

You get out of education what you put into it, and parents can do a lot to supplement their child's education no matter what school they attend. But this is one area where most parents need help. Chances are their own career experience has been pretty limited, too.

Having experienced my own midlife career crisis, though, I feel keenly that we need to do more than show kids what subjects they test well in. We need to get more hands-on experiences into kids' hands.

My school had a beautiful career center that too often sat empty. Kids' days were packed too full to spend much time there. And truthfully, many kids just aren't motivated enough to spend their spare time researching careers if it's not required.

A few fortunate kids start college knowing exactly what they want to be when they grow up. But most don't. Many of my former students tell me they're biding time in college, worrying about the day they'll have to declare a major. Some go on to graduate school simply because they don't know what to do next.

If there were more time in a student's schedule for career exploration, from grade school on up, maybe school would seem more relevant to kids. And if school were more relevant, maybe grade point averages and test scores would go up.

We teach kids the skills they need to join the workforce. But we're so busy testing them on those skills that we're ignoring what they'll do with those skills when they leave us. A rich, thriving career program will result in happier students—and ultimately, happier adults.

As for my own career crisis? Well, way back in 1975 I spent a day-on-the-job at *The Flint Journal*.

Sometimes things really do come full circle.

CHAPTER 9

Politics and Legislation

NCLB: DID CONGRESS EVEN BOTHER TO READ THE DAMN THING BEFORE THEY VOTED ON IT?

Is My School Really Failing?

Come with me.

I'm going to take you inside a Phase 5 school, aka a "failing" school because it has not made adequate yearly progress under the requirements of the federal No Child Left Behind Act (NCLB).

I'm withholding the name of the school because, frankly, their morale can't take another hit. The name doesn't matter, though, because the story is the same at most of the so-called failing schools.

This school has a 47 percent mobility rate. Though it's kept quiet, 10 to 15 percent of the families are homeless. They stay with this friend, or that relative, until they are asked to leave.

The parents mostly fall into three categories: grandparents raising their grandchildren, parents who had their children when they were fourteen or fifteen years old, and foster parents.

Many of the students start kindergarten not knowing their colors, numbers, or alphabet. Some don't even know their own names, having been called nicknames like "Boo" their whole lives. Many cannot pick their own name out of a list, let alone write it. Many have never seen a book. They have no understanding even of the left-to-right concept in reading.

Behavior is the number one problem here. Watching a fourth grade class being taught multiplication, you'd think that the entire class has attention deficit disorder. They wiggle and tap, rip paper, eyes roaming, looking for someone to poke or prod. They cannot focus and they cannot keep still. They also cannot multiply.

Defiance is the word of the day, every day. Their lives are about street survival. School is inconsequential. Teachers tread carefully—how much can you prod a student before they rebel: "I'm not doing that and you can't make me."

Anger reigns. Fists are the only way they know to settle disputes, and they use them freely. The ones who won't fight must be closely guarded by teachers or their pencils and lunch money will be stolen.

Parents were invited to the school to learn strategies to help their children prepare for the state standardized test. After a great deal of begging, six to ten parents finally showed up. First, they had to be taught how to multiply.

For the next two weeks, not only the students will be tested. The staff will be tested too, because students will go out of their way to get into trouble, to be suspended, to avoid having to take The Test.

During the math lesson, no fourth grader can figure out 63 x 2. Yet this week when students face the test they will be asked questions like, "Max is at the carnival. He wants to play the Ball Toss. When he tosses the ball, it will land in one of the numbered rings: 25, 50, or 100. In his first game, Max will toss six balls at the rings. What is the lowest score he could get if the ball always lands in a numbered ring?"

So, will this be the year they pass the test?

What do you think?

Know of What You Speak

So how do those 30-second television spots work for ya, anyway? Do they tell you what you need to know about the candidates?

Not me. I don't believe all that down-home posturing. Politicians with the kind of money it takes to run a campaign probably don't relate much to the public they serve.

Which is why, as a teacher, it infuriated me every time those politicians made decisions that affected my students and me. Other than stump speeches, photo ops, or a quick read of "The Pet Goat," most political candidates haven't set foot in a school since they were students themselves.

But education is fundamental to our success as a society. Education policy is one of the most significant things an elected official will ever do.

Personally, I think we need a better system. Simply analyzing student data and test scores doesn't cut it. The policy makers need to meet the kids, in the trenches.

So, to prove they're highly qualified, I propose that all political candidates be required to complete the PREP Internship (Politician's "Real Experience" Primer). Unpaid, of course.

Here's how it would work.

To qualify, aspiring politicians must take every grade level of state-mandated tests in every subject. Their scores will be published in the newspaper, where they will be analyzed and compared to other candidates' scores. Didn't make adequate progress? One retake allowed.

Once they've passed the state-mandated tests, they will enter a school district for one semester, much like a student teacher. No grandstanding allowed.

Because funding cuts in schools have a domino effect, the political interns will perform a variety of jobs so that they understand the impact of such cuts—work the cafeteria line, observe guidance counseling sessions, shadow the school nurse for a day.

Children's attitudes and behavior speak volumes about their home lives. To that end, political interns will spend one week with custodians cleaning the cafeteria after lunch. The shocking waste of food and the rudeness of students will teach them a great deal about their voters.

They will drive a school bus for a week and break up fights at the bus stop. This provides the added bonus of experiencing the roads in their district and seeing where their voters live.

They will prepare and deliver several units of state test preparation for each level—elementary, middle, and high school. Papers, of course, must be graded at home at night.

They will sit through several long curriculum meetings and attend parent–teacher conferences, in a building with no air on an 80-degree day. They will accommodate the requests of those parents, no matter how absurd, and answer to parents threatening lawsuits—without legal representation, of course. One week will be spent making home visits with social workers, solving family problems, and finding funding when necessary.

For the written portion of the internship, they will create a budget for a first year teacher (with spouse and child) that includes finding the time and money for mandated graduate classes.

Politician as public servant?

Oh, please. They don't know the meaning of the term until they've worked in a public school.

Don't Call Me a Bigot

One of the most insulting things ever said to me—and I'm including myself in this group because I was still a classroom teacher when he said it—was when President George W. Bush said that educators practice the "soft bigotry of low expectations."

Whoa. That's ugly. Worst case, he flat-out called us bigots who are prejudiced against minorities and low income students. Best case, he said that we expect less from some students because of their backgrounds.

His loathsome insinuation is that educators look at the color of students' skin, their economic status, or their background, and assume that they cannot learn—an idea that is as repugnant to me as I'm sure it is to my colleagues. It goes against everything that I believe about children and learning and my role as a teacher.

I'll tell you what teachers do look at, though. We look at the skills a student brings to our class, usually by giving a pretest. Then we look at what that child is supposed to know by the time they complete our class. And sometimes it's just too much. The gap is too great to be bridged in one year.

It's not bigotry. It's not low expectations. It's fact.

We don't believe that disadvantaged children can't learn. Of course they can. But if they come to us from a family that uses a vocabulary limited to slang, a home where English is a second language, or where so little reading is done that the child doesn't even know which direction to turn the pages of a book, those children are going to have a hard time catching up to grade level in the short time we have them. But they can still make great strides in their learning.

The Educational Testing Service sponsored a survey of parents, educators, and the general public, conducted jointly by the polling firms of Peter D. Hart (Democrat) and David Winston (Republican). Predictably, the results were manipulated and taken out of context by pundits looking to support their own views, and to pit teachers against the public on the subject of education reform.

For example, 55 percent of the public said that students, teachers, and schools should be held to the same performance standards even if they come from disadvantaged backgrounds. However, not surprisingly, 60 percent of teachers disagreed. This difference, the result of teachers looking at students as individuals, is where the so-called soft bigotry comes in.

So how should student learning be measured? On how much each student learns over time? Or on achievement, meaning what they know compared to a firm standard (other students their age)? Teachers, administrators, and the public almost overwhelmingly agree that a combination of the two methods would be best. Yet, most standardized tests measure achievement only.

The soft bigotry of low expectations? I don't think so. Sounds more like the warm tolerance of individual progress, if you ask me.

NCLB: Tutoring and Transfers

Something's missing. Something big. The most sweeping education reform ever has a big, fat hole in it.

Education Secretary Margaret Spellings took public schools to task because only a fraction of students took advantage of the options for free tutoring or transfers out of failing schools, provisions of the No Child Left Behind Act. Less than 20 percent of eligible students signed up for free tutoring, and less than 1 percent of eligible students actually transferred to other schools. She contends that they were not made aware of their choices.

I don't think that's the whole story.

Think for a moment about the so-called failing schools. Most are in urban areas of blight and poverty. There is a reason that the students at those schools are failing, but it's not because they can't learn.

In urban areas, often students fail because education is the farthest thing from their minds as they cope with day-to-day survival. Financial, physical, social, mental, and emotional survival. Poverty, drugs, gangs, street life, homelessness—these are not just words for them. They are a seemingly inescapable way of life.

Many kids raised in a culture of failure think that what goes on at school—education—has nothing to do with them. And in all fairness, it probably doesn't, not in any immediate sense. It doesn't protect them from the gangs in their neighborhood. It doesn't pay for a doctor if they get sick. It doesn't get the drug pusher off their corner. It doesn't give their mom a job. It doesn't put food in the refrigerator. It doesn't get their dad off drugs or out of jail. School is irrelevant to them in a huge way.

That's what's missing from NCLB. The human element.

Why on earth would students sign up for after-school tutoring when they don't do their regular schoolwork? Why on earth would they go to the trouble to get the voucher (yes, it *is* a voucher) to transfer to another school, when they've been absent more days than not in the school they're enrolled in now?

It's not low expectations. No one's telling them they can't succeed. No one's telling them anything, because they aren't there to hear it.

Yes, even in "failing" schools in bad neighborhoods there are motivated kids who care about their education and who will take advantage of tutoring or transfers. For them, the options work.

There's a lot we can do to improve the educational system in this country. But NCLB is an incomplete solution. NCLB is about rules and regulations and tests and statistics and paperwork and politics. It does not address, never even *mentions*, the mindset, the culture, of the nonlearner.

So are some kids going to be left behind? Sadly, yes. And NCLB has nothing to offer that will fix that.

Big Business Cashes In on Your School's "Failure"

If your school is labeled as failing, big business will be laughing—all the way to the bank.

Because even though the voucher provision did not officially make it into the No Child Left Behind Act, like a pedophile in a clown suit, it's lurking in there.

If a school is labeled as "in improvement," school officials must inform parents that they are eligible for school money for private remedial services—up to $1,500 per child. In other words, NCLB allows Title I federal tax dollars to be moved out of public schools and into for-profit, non-profit, or faith-based supplemental service providers.

They call it a supplemental services opportunity.

I call it reinventing the wheel.

Before I got my teaching job I worked as a private tutor. One of my students was a tenth grader named Sam, referred to me by his English teacher. Sam was a smart kid, but he had a hard time concentrating in class. I had worked with Sam only four times when I got a call from his English teacher.

"Sam did so well on his last writing assignment—you didn't write it for him did you?" she asked. I assured her that of course I had not. What Sam needed, I told her, was simply a personal explanation of the assignment, and some one-on-one instruction in writing. In that one-on-one scenario, Sam flourished.

Which is exactly what educators have been saying forever. Kids learn better in small classes because they get more individual attention.

So along comes the underfunded No Child Left Behind Act, which uses one measurement—a test—and sets impossibly high standards. If a school does not make adequate yearly progress, which happens for many reasons beyond the district's control (English as a second language, large numbers of special education students, too few students taking the test), they get slapped with an ugly and unfair label. To add insult to injury, they must then give money to parents to hire a supplemental service provider to do what the public school was not funded to do in the first place.

Wouldn't it make more sense to simply provide enough money to schools and require that they lower their student–teacher ratio? Of course it would. But guess who would lose out then? Big business. And big business controls the political power. Politicos would rather see that money go to private companies such as Sylvan Learning.

And what, exactly, makes Sylvan centers so successful with students? It's simple—they boast a 3:1 student–teacher ratio. That student–teacher ratio allows them to individualize learning in a way that large class sizes don't.

Sylvan Learning is one of the largest tutoring providers in North America. And the madness of NCLB ensures that they, and similar businesses, will thrive in the years to come.

The political machine that has orchestrated deregulation at every turn is suddenly regulating every facet of public education.

I don't care what you call it. A voucher by any other name is still a voucher.

Everyone's Accountable— Except Big Business

It's the height of hypocrisy.

The battle cry of the No Child Left Behind Act has been a raucous rebel yell of "accountability, accountability, accountability!" And unnerved public school systems have scrambled to meet that call, throwing aside their own school improvement plans and the time and money they've spent on them, to meet a new set of criteria set by people far removed from the unique culture of each school.

And first and foremost on the NCLB accountability agenda is The Test.

NCLB mandates have resulted in approximately forty-five million standardized tests a year. The tests are huge high stakes for students and schools, and low scores can deem a school a failure, deny a student's promotion, and destroy his self-esteem.

With so much at stake it's more than troubling that test companies operate with almost no regulation. The $2 billion-a-year testing industry, like all industry, is most concerned with its bottom line. It would be foolish to think otherwise, to think that test companies are concerned about education, not profit. And because the priority is profit, why would they do any more than is required of them by law?

And precious little is required. There is no independent agency overseeing the for-profit testing industry. And the very nature of the industry—keeping tests and answer keys under wraps—makes it difficult to monitor, easy to hide mistakes.

There have been plenty of mistakes. Little regulation combined with an exploding testing market has resulted in late test results and serious errors. In Minnesota, hundreds of students were unfairly denied diplomas because of scoring errors. And 4,100 teachers were told they failed certification tests that they had actually passed. Examples abound, but one has to wonder, how many scoring errors were not caught?

Another piece in the accountability game is teacher quality. Teachers are accountable, too, forced to meet new criteria to become "highly qualified." Veteran teachers are spending their own time and money to take more college classes, pass certification tests, and rack up professional development hours.

Meanwhile, if a school does not make adequate yearly progress, it must hand over Title I funds (that's a voucher, folks), which students can take to an unregulated, for-profit tutoring store, or an online service, and pay to be tutored by an untrained, noncertified tutor. Little oversight of the tutoring industry leaves the door wide open for fly-by-night companies to take advantage of lucrative tutoring contracts.

Does this make sense to you?

The testing and tutoring industries are enjoying record profits as a result of NCLB. But more important, the two industries are key to the futures and reputations of students, schools, and staff across the country.

With so much riding on these two industries, it's not too much to ask that they be held accountable, too.

NCLB Leaves Gifted and Talented Behind

They're leaving all kinds of children behind. Don't think for a minute they're not.

The No Child Left Behind Act, that sweeping education legislation that is supposed to save children from the alleged incompetence and inequity of the public school system, leaves behind the very students who could some day lead the world.

I'm referring to "gifted and talented" students, also called "high ability learners." NCLB offers nothing to meet their needs.

A bounty of services is provided for special education students. I once attended an Individualized Education Program (IEP) meeting that included a general education teacher, special ed. teacher, psychologist, social worker, teacher consultant, special education director, counselor, behavior specialist, director of student support services, one student, two parents, and a principal. Ten professionals all focused on the needs of one student.

Federal law requires annual IEPs for every special education student, though not all are so heavily attended. But it's a telling example of the kind of time, money, and effort that is routinely spent on special education.

Why don't gifted students deserve equal protection under the law? No federal or state funding is mandated for high ability learners. Services to meet their needs are considered to be "luxury" programs. When money gets tight, those programs are the first to go.

The federal government spends billions of dollars on special education. It requires school districts to provide every possible service a child could need: in-home teachers, communication devices, personal aides, anything.

Yet the U.S. Department of Education complains mightily that American students need to focus more on the STEM fields—science, technology, engineering, and math—if they're to compete globally.

So where's the money? Why do we provide absolutely every service imaginable for special education students, but provide almost nothing for students at the other end of the spectrum? Why doesn't the government value the potential of these high ability students and what they might do for our global competitiveness? Why doesn't the government mandate and pay for a gifted program in every school? Why didn't the authors of NCLB address the needs of high ability learners?

Is it possible that gifted students are just pawns in a bigger picture?

Because the result of the inequity is this: With no programs in place hundreds of gifted students go unidentified. The parents of children identified as gifted end up frustrated because they're not challenged in school. So they turn to charters and private schools, two pet projects of this presidential administration.

Is it a stretch to imagine that the negligence toward high ability learners is part of a plot to dismantle the public school system?

Perhaps. But one thing's for sure: eventually most of those gifted students take their high test scores, and leave the public school behind.

The McGraw–Bush Connection

On his first day in the White House, President George W. Bush reportedly invited longtime family friend Harold McGraw III, of the McGraw-Hill Companies, into his office. Two days later Bush introduced to Congress the No Child Left Behind Act. I'm thinking the conversation went something like this . . .

"Look at that White House lawn, Georgie. All that green."

"Speaking of green, Harry, how's things at McGraw-Hill Companies? Shareholders happy?"

"I'm glad you asked, Georgie—."

"Anything I can do to help, Harry, you know that. Our daddies and granddaddies have been helping each other since the 1930s."

"Well, that Reading First program you pushed when you were the governor of Texas was solid gold for us, Georgie. We got our curriculum materials into nearly every Texas school, thanks to your requirement that they use 'scientifically valid' research. We were happy to provide that research, too.

"But I've got a plan that will establish you as the education president, and make McGraw-Hill's profits soar.

"First, Georgie, my boy, you tell Congress you want to eliminate the nation's reading deficit. Get with our favorite testing lobbyist Sandy Kress to design some new education legislation, something with a real nice ring to it, something that even the bleeding hearts have to accept because they'll look heartless if they don't.

"Now you make this legislation big, like over a thousand pages, so that no one will bother to read the whole dang thing before they pass it.

"Georgie, you tell them you'll be real generous with the money, as long as the instructional practices are 'scientifically based,' but you'll withhold funding if they're not. We'll dig up some more 'experts' to provide that research.

"Then you get your people to launch a campaign to point out every single thing the public school systems are doing wrong, how all these poor kids are just at their mercy. You know, point out how the minorities aren't doing as well as the majority, that sort of thing. Make it sound like you're going to level the playing field. Hire some hungry pundits to spread the word for you.

"Once you've planted the seed that the public school system is an abysmal mess, roll out your solution."

"My solution?! Harry, I don't have—."

"Sure you do, Georgie. You've got the perfect solution. First you take your Texas literacy plan nationwide, and get our reading curriculum into every school. And then—this part's genius—you test them, every grade K–12. My company will provide the tests. Hell, we'll even provide the materials to teach to those tests!"

"Wha—?!"

"It's like this, Georgie. All you have to do is convince the public that a good education boils down to textbooks and tests. That's it.

"You create the demand, Georgie. McGraw-Hill will handle the supply."

It's the Students, Stupid

On my desk sits a three-inch stack of articles about the No Child Left Behind Act. I've been researching NCLB until I'm bobbly-eyed and numb. In fact, I've done more reading about education in the last month than I did in my entire twenty-year teaching career. The truth is, when you teach you're so immersed in the actual teaching that you rarely have time to read educational theory.

And it's clear to me that it's just that: theory. It's been a real eye-opener, this delve into what the latest "experts" have to say about education. The one thing I keep searching for just isn't there.

What I want to know is, where are the kids in all of this? I have read the opinion of every kind of "educational expert" from every kind of organization I can find, but except as a number in a test score, I can't find the students, the key piece in the education puzzle.

The experts have all kinds of solutions: disaggregate the data and look at each ethnicity, administer this test instead of that, align the curriculum, raise the standards and benchmarks, make teachers more qualified, allow kids to leave failing schools. But all of the "solutions" leave out one crucial thing.

They leave out the lazy factor.

The lazy factor is something teachers are intimately acquainted with. It's one of the main reasons kids fail. Ask any teacher, and she'll tell you that if a kid tries, he'll usually learn.

In the hall outside my classroom I've had hundreds of frustrating conversations like this one.

> Me: "Johnny, you are such a bright kid. You are so smart. You have so much talent. There are so many things you are good at. Why won't you do your schoolwork?"
>
> Johnny: (*shrugs*)
>
> Me: "Can you tell me why you won't do your work?"
>
> Johnny: (*shrugs again*)
>
> Me: "I talked to some of your other teachers. They tell me the same thing, that you're intelligent, but you just won't apply yourself. What can we do to help?"
>
> Johnny: (*stares off into space*)
>
> Me: "Johnny, I've talked to your parents. They say they can't get you to do your work either. Why? Help me out here. Isn't there something that interests you? Do you want to be an E student? Your academic records make you *look* dumb, but you're *not*!"
>
> Johnny: (*sighs*)
>
> Me: "Johnny, do you want to grow up to *be* dumb?!"

Many years ago, I voiced this frustration to our assistant principal. She explained that in junior high and high school, it's all about physical and social growth. There's very little brain growth.

Well, guess what? A study by the scientists at the National Institute on Alcohol Abuse and Alcoholism says just that. They have discovered a biological excuse for laziness. Apparently, adolescents between the ages of twelve and seventeen have half the blood flow of adults in the area of their brains that governs drive.

The politicians who come up with education reform must picture kids sitting at attention at their desks, hands folded neatly, yes ma'aming and no ma'aming like some 1950s TV series. It's rarely like that, though.

Even the most inspiring, gifted teachers struggle with the lazy factor. It's the thing that makes teachers want to shriek when they collect homework at the beginning of the hour and only half of the kids turn it in. It's the thing that has teachers slumped over their desks at the end of the day as they enter grades in their record books.

Give me a kid who is eager to learn, and I can work wonders with that child. But give me a lazy kid, a kid who could care less about learning, and I can't guarantee anything.

With or without NCLB.

What the Heck Do You Know About Good Teaching?

I'll just say it flat out: I know a couple of teachers who have absolutely no business in a classroom. I know it, their students know it, and administrators in their district know it. Yet, for whatever reason, the rigorous evaluation procedures that are in place to get rid of bad teachers aren't used.

They aren't bad teachers because they don't know their subject; they're bad teachers because they're lazy, or disorganized, or mean to kids.

That's why the Highly Qualified Teacher provision of the No Child Left Behind Act is so absurd. It implies that the one thing that's going to ensure a good teacher in every classroom is requiring that teachers have a major in the subject they teach. And that's just not true.

Yes, subject mastery is important. But good teaching is more complex than that. A huge part of good teaching is an even disposition. A sense of humor helps. A warm countenance, concern for kids, fairness, militant organizational skills, unflagging energy, a true understanding of how people learn, and the ability to explain things in multiple ways are vital, too. Yet the new legislation addresses none of that.

Some subjects require more material mastery than others, say math, or Advanced Placement courses. But a true teacher can teach almost anything.

What galls me about NCLB is that the suits in Washington gather a few stats, then make decisions and pass legislation with nary a clue as to how it will actually play out inside the walls of a school or a classroom.

This legislation has the potential to devastate small school districts where teachers sometimes teach a few classes in their major and a few in their minor, because there aren't enough sections to allow them to teach only their major. So now what? Drop them to part-time? Hire more part-timers? Consolidate with other districts to create mega-schools? Oh, yeah, that's good for kids.

Layoffs are possible, too, but it won't necessarily be the "unqualified" teachers who are laid off. If a teacher would rather switch to his major than go to the time and expense of changing his minor to a major, school officials may have to move him to someone else's position.

It's one thing to tighten the requirements for new hires (though still causing hardship for small schools). But a grandfather clause should protect veteran teachers from spending their own time and money to prove they can do what they've been doing for years.

Here's what one teacher told me: "I have a bachelor of science degree in physics, so I am a trained research physicist according to Michigan State University. I prefer teaching in my math minor, but I am not considered 'highly qualified' despite having a math class every semester in college above and beyond calculus. You'd think that a major like physics, which is based entirely upon mathematical models, would make me highly qualified in math."

I've heard dozens of stories like that. The legislation is illogical, ineffective, and it won't raise kids' test scores. It diverts time and money away from the classroom where it is needed most. It certainly doesn't address the heart of good teaching.

NCLB takes control from states and local school districts and puts it into the hands of the federal government. I would much rather answer to the parents of my students, who know me and see what I'm doing in the classroom, than to a bunch of politicians who only set foot inside a school when it's time to deliver a stump speech.

It's crazy. Why on earth would we accept the definition of "highly qualified" from people so far removed from schools?

Just Ordinary People
with Extraordinary Heart

Okay, so all teachers aren't perfect.

A lot of us are just plain ordinary. Competent, yes. But fairly average, too.

What can you do about that, though? If you look around you, wherever you work, there probably aren't very many truly extraordinary employees.

The highly qualified requirements address a teacher's knowledge of subject. But as you know, a teacher can know her subject backward and forward and still be a really bad teacher.

When I think of the bad teachers I know, they're not bad because they don't know their material. In fact, I don't know any teachers who don't know their material. The bad teachers I know antagonize kids. They're mean-spirited and impatient and indifferent. The bad teachers I know have unimaginative lesson plans. They think that being right is more important than being kind. They're lazy and disorganized and unwilling to try something new.

But the best teachers I know? The best teachers are firm, but warm. Inspiring and creative. Organized, yet flexible. They're funny and fun and quick to laugh—even at themselves.

You can't legislate that.

That's why the highly qualified legislation in NCLB misses the mark. It boils good teaching down to credentials on paper.

I've had a lot of years to listen to teacher bashers, and I get plenty of e-mails from them now. When people complain about public schools in general, and teachers specifically, I can't help but think, "Okay, so what's your solution? To fire them all? Then what? Where are you going to find enough teachers, let alone enough extraordinary teachers, to fill those positions?"

I mean, the human pool is filled with pretty average people.

If they fired every teacher today and replaced them, the new teachers would face exactly the same problems in the classroom. They're just ordinary people, too.

I've had a few extraordinary teachers in my lifetime. So have you. But only a few. Yet we want our children's teachers to be all extraordinary, all the time.

I get that. I want that, too.

I just don't know how realistic it is.

And I don't have an answer. But I do know that teacher bashing doesn't work. Disdain and antagonism toward teachers just makes them defensive. And if they're busy being defensive, they aren't at their best.

That's what bugs me about education reform. Often it's more about blame than support.

With student enrollment rising in most districts, and experts predicting we'll need more than two million new teachers in the next decade, we need to work with teachers, not against them.

So instead of passing legislation that looks good on paper, but is really about a political agenda, we need education reform that gets to the heart of good teaching.

Because that's what good teaching is—all heart.

NCLB Lets Buildings Crumble

Most of the kids I know have plenty of stuff. They have cell phones and iPods and TVs in their bedrooms. Even in the very poor school districts I've visited, most kids wear expensive athletic shoes and talk about the DVDs they watched at home.

What too many kids don't have, though, is an appreciation for the value of education.

And we have no one to blame but ourselves.

In this country we send a very strong and clear message that education is not important. It's not as important as another country's democracy or big businesses' profits or an individual legislator's pork.

Need proof? Just follow the money.

I've had the opportunity to visit dozens of schools in the last five years. A few were beautiful. Most were plain and institutional. And too many were crumbling, ugly, and downright dangerous.

School districts lucky enough to have money for building improvement often are forced to spend it reactively rather than proactively. They play catch-up, fixing things as they break, or on necessities like safety and security. They rarely have the luxury of designing and building the perfect school—a school with student achievement in mind.

But a community in Manassas, Virginia, did. Manassas Park High School was built with intention. According to an Associated Press story, every single facet of the building was designed to improve student achievement and behavior. What's intriguing is the attention to detail—details that perhaps only someone who's worked in a school can appreciate.

For example, bathroom mirrors are in the hall, instead of in the bathroom. That may sound silly to you, but it makes perfect sense to me. The mirror is the main reason most kids go into a school bathroom. It's the thing that keeps them in there forever, too. They cluster around it and primp, giggle or fight, away from adult supervision. Putting the mirror in the hall is pure genius.

And the intention is paying off. Scores in algebra, geometry, and writing have jumped since the building opened in 1999. School officials credit that attention to detail, including roomier chairs, window shades that block glare but still let in indirect light, and a floor plan that is safe without being prison-like.

Teachers know how much something as simple as room temperature can affect students: too warm and they're sleepy, too cold and they complain—relentlessly. Neither, of course, is conducive to learning.

Ironically, NCLB, touted as being the most comprehensive school reform ever, demands improved student achievement without addressing a fundamental element that hinders student learning—the embarrassing state of many of our country's school buildings.

So the question is, how can we expect Johnny to value education if he must dodge buckets in the hall that catch water from the leaky roof, or watch his teacher smack the radiator to get it going, or suffer the annoying flicker of florescent lights all day long?

Unfortunately, I think, we already have our answer.

Stop Telling Me What I Need (And Don't Give Me What You Need)

Riiiing!

"Hello, Mrs. Olmstead, sixth grade teacher speaking."

"Hel-*lo*, this is Glen Gladhander, your state legislator, and boy, have I got good news for you! We've got $39 million in our state budget agreement that will revolutionize education. In fact, it's going to make you a more effective teacher and bring your students full speed into the age of technology."

"Wow! Really? Does that mean I'm finally getting—"

"Yes, ma'am, are you ready for this?! We're going to give every sixth grader in the state *a laptop computer*!"

"Ah. A laptop. Every sixth grader. Wow. Well, thank you. That's very generous of you. I assume you surveyed teachers to see what they—"

"Generous is my middle name! Nothing's too good for education in my state! By second semester every child in your class will have a shiny new laptop! In fact, in six years all middle and high school students will have laptops, too!"

"Sounds wonderful. Who, exactly, is responsible for them? Can the kids take them home?"

"Home, church, vacation, you name it, honey!"

"So the kids will have to tote them around . . . their backpacks are full and heavy as it is . . . hmmm . . . if they don't take them home, where, exactly, will I keep them? My classroom's small, and my one cabinet that locks isn't big enough to hold thirty laptops."

"Well, sweetie, you might just have to get yourself some new cabinets."

"And you know, just because each child has a laptop doesn't mean they'll have Internet access at home."

"Then they'll hook 'em up in your classroom."

"Great. So they'll be putting Internet access in my classroom? Can my district afford that? And what about electricity? Our tech people keep telling us that our building is old and the wiring isn't equipped to handle so many computers. Will they rewire the whole building? And will the laptops be networked?"

"Networks? Ah . . . maybe CNN . . ."

"Hmmm . . . I see. Well, kids lose stuff *all* the time. What happens when they lose it? It's not exactly like losing your textbook, you know. I won't be able to just hand them another one. If we're doing a lesson on the laptop, what about the kids who forgot it at home?"

"Well, uh—"

"And what about theft? What happens when Johnny gets his laptop stolen?"

"Well, uh—"

"And what about repairs? Kids are hard on equipment. Is money allocated for maintenance and repairs? And what about kids who break them repeatedly? What do they do while their laptop is being repaired?"

"Well, little lady, you're a smart girl, I'm sure you'll figure that out."

"Well, what about upgrades? In a few years, the laptops this first class gets will be outdated. Then what?"

"Well, we'll just cross that bridge when we come to it. Don't you worry about that now, you let *me* worry about that!"

"And when will I be trained on how to implement the laptop into my curriculum? I mean, summer's almost over so it's too late to do it now. And once school starts there's so little time for intensive training. How will I?"

"Curricu-what?"

"The curriculum. It's so full already there's no room to add anything extra. I have to work the laptops into what we're already covering . . ."

"Like I said, you're a real smart cookie. Why, with all the education you got, you'll figure that out in a snap!"

"Riiight. Will they be equipped with programs that fit into my curriculum? Will they help me meet the state standards and benchmarks? I mean, the kids will just fill them up with games if you let them. It could end up being a very expensive game toy."

"Stands, benches, games? We talkin' stadiums here? How 'bout Detroit's Comerica Park—!"

"I'm sorry, sir, I certainly don't want to seem ungrateful, but there are a lot of things that—"

"Okay, missy, gotta run. I got a meeting with some guys from IBM, then lunch with Tigers' owner Mike Ilitch. Tigers have finally improved since we built them that new stadium. Maybe we can free up a few dollars for the Lions. . ."

CHAPTER 10

Take Back the Profession

WE'RE THE EXPERTS ON
TEACHING AND LEARNING

Let's Get a Little Rowdy

Out of the mouths of babes . . .

Students in the Atherton school district in Flint, Michigan, protested the cutting of 8.5 teaching positions by pulling a fire alarm and swarming out of the building.

Shortly after, I was invited by those same students to visit their school. For two hours I listened to kids despair over what might be cut from their education: Band? Yearbook? Eight or nine of their beloved teachers? The concern was different for each student.

Impressed by their intensity, yet despairing myself over what piece of their education might land on the sacrificial altar, I started thinking . . . *what if?*

What if the grown-ups followed their lead? What if we all got a little rowdy, a little out of line, and every single person from the biggest city to the smallest village came together in one big synchronized protest of the current funding of education? What if we stomped our feet as one and said firmly to our legislators, "No. That's not good enough."

I also started thinking about a little Econ lesson I saw on the Internet, where Ben Cohen of Ben and Jerry's ice cream explains the federal budget using Oreo cookies at www.truemajority.com. In it, he demonstrates how education could be adequately funded by simply moving a drop of money from the gargantuan defense budget into the education budget.

I know that every district faces budget cuts, all the time. That's exactly my point. Every district across the country sits in the same sinking boat, making cold, hard decisions about what to throw overboard.

But what if we just said "no"? Imagine the power if kids all across the country worked together to protest cuts to their education? And what if their parents joined them?

What if, on the same day, at the same time, all across the country, we protested in school parking lots, in front of grocery stores, on street corners, and in the town square, carried signs and handed out flyers, just like a march on Washington but in our own hometowns, complete with media coverage? What if we sent a strong, clear message to our elected officials that we're fed up, and we're not going to take it any more?

Because, you see, I don't believe that the money isn't there. Not for a minute. Legislators are just choosing to spend your money on something other than education, and you're letting them. You can bet that if their choices were going to cost them their jobs as elected officials, they'd take a cold, hard look at their priorities and make some different decisions.

It's up to us. It's always been up to us, we just forget that sometimes. We hold the power in our voting hands. We can choose to be an enlightened society that puts education first.

Or not.

Call me naive, but I still believe in the power of the people.

I say, it's time to get a little rowdy.

I dare you.

I double-dog dare you.

We're Not Gonna Take It, Any More

It had nothing to do with Matthew McConaughey on a Caribbean island but, nerd that I am, my fantasy finally came true.

On June 21, 2004, I joined over eleven thousand educators, parents, and students on a march to the Michigan state capital in support of bold legislation that addressed the funding needs of K–16 education. They came from almost every county in the state, representing over 387 school districts.

It was about time.

They say that in the last twenty-five years of politics in Lansing no crowd that large ever marched in support of anything. I'm not surprised. I've always believed that if teachers mobilized their extraordinary organizational skills they could rule the world.

As we poured down Michigan Avenue and onto the front lawn of the capitol building, I knew I was part of something huge. And though our personalities might be as different as the communities we teach in, on that day every single one of us was on the same page.

Oh, the power of collective thought.

They say there's safety in numbers, power in knowledge, might in right. If that's true, then that particular group of people was brilliant beyond belief and powerful beyond imagining.

In all honesty, I've often been impatient with the people of my profession. I've felt they were too easily placated, too timid, too willing to play by the rules when it was clear that no one else was. I know they're not apathetic. I know they're simply consumed with the activity inside the walls of their classrooms.

But on that day, they shined. In comfortable clothes and sensible shoes, carrying umbrellas and brown bag lunches, astoundingly good-natured in spite of the wicked heat, they made a profound statement simply by being themselves.

Like Dorothy, they've had the power all along.

As I stood sweating under that scorching sun, I felt the power of that wholesome, steadfast group. And I felt hope—hope that the power of us, the ones who value education above all else, coupled with the power of them, our employees at the state capitol, could get it done. I hoped that with firm and relentless pressure we could say to those "other" legislators, the ones who would not come out on the capitol steps to greet us, "This is it. This is your final reprimand. Fund education properly or you'll be looking for a new job."

The challenge, after an extraordinary event like that, is to keep the momentum going after everyone scatters back to real life—curriculum meetings, paper grading, parent conferences, and student discipline. The challenge is not to let the power of that brilliant moment in the blazing sun, become a distant memory.

Because it's all within our reach if we want it. Don't forget—legislators work for us.

So tell them. Choose education for kids.

The Bottom Line

I used to walk down the halls of the high school during my planning hour, peeking into each classroom I passed, amazed at all of the cool lessons going on, soaking up the feel of the place, marveling at the single-minded dedication of my colleagues as they presented material to students.

The door of each classroom framed a snapshot: Kids with heads bent over microscopes studying amoebas. Kids crowded around the physics teacher as he demonstrated a law of motion. Kids giggling at themselves as they stumbled over the words of Shakespeare. Kids' faces tight with concentration as they worked out quadratic equations in geometry.

There's this magical feeling in a high school when classes are in session, teachers are teaching, and students are learning. The school sort of thrums and pulsates with a low-level hum, almost a buzz.

What is this gentle buzz? I used to wonder. Why does this feel so holy, so sacred?

And then I realized. It's not the school. It's not the teachers. It's not even the students that create the buzz. The buzz is what happens when you put the three together.

The buzz is the Pursuit of Knowledge.

And that's where every piece of education legislation goes astray—by revering the outcome rather than the pursuit.

And so I say to you, let us resolve to hold the pursuit of knowledge as a sacred trust. Let us resolve to approach this pursuit with the same reverence one would show to a sacrament.

For it is the *pursuit* that is the deity. Not the test scores. Not the grade point average. Not the rating by Standard & Poor's. It's the pursuit itself, the effort, the endeavor, the *attempt* to learn that should be venerated.

All learning is valuable, but the learning that takes place in the primary and secondary school settings is especially sacrosanct, because the students are all initiates. They're here because they have to be, not by choice. These first experiences will shape how they approach the pursuit of knowledge for the rest of their lives.

And because what they experience here will determine how they feel about learning for the rest of their lives, every single detail of their experience here should be executed with the utmost care and treated with reverence.

It's almost a given that people will go out of their way to help a pregnant woman or a child in need. It's an unspoken understanding that for the most part, our society protects the vulnerable.

So it should be for schools and those in them, from the superintendent to the custodian, because they are all part of a grand, magnificent ceremony.

It should be the collective effort of every person to place the education of our youth at the very top of the priority list because that is the key to success for our society, our future, our planet.

Until every person in every community makes it his or her business to treat the educational system with reverence, we won't "fix" education.

Imagine a world where people bow their heads in reverence upon entering a school.

Imagine a world where people genuflect toward the textbooks that hold the information that will teach our children to read and write.

Imagine a world where people give freely to schools when the collection plate is passed.

Once the pursuit of knowledge is considered to be sacred, the rest will fall into place.

Amen.

Epilogue

One of the things that made me crazy when I taught was how little input I had into things that directly affected me in the classroom. It seemed that everyone had a voice in what I was doing except me. Politicians. Parents. "Experts." People who hadn't set foot in a school since they were students themselves were making policies that affected my students and me. They didn't know what was best for us, but I was told over and over that they did.

Legislators continue to make decisions about education policy without input from the very people standing in front of the students, the true experts in teaching and learning. "Studies" and "reports" that come out of partisan think tanks are given more credence than input from real teachers in real classrooms. The media, fed by private interest groups and politicians with an agenda, have painted a picture of teachers, and the schools they teach in, as slovenly, unqualified, ill-equipped, and self-serving. One of the biggest challenges for educators is to not believe their own bad press. The other is to change it.

Standing in the buffet line at a Fourth of July barbecue, an acquaintance said to me: "I used to read the newspaper and wonder what in the world was going on in the public schools. I just couldn't figure out what had gone so wrong. It sounded like they were in a shambles. Then I got a job with the Jackson Public Schools, and I see now that public schools are persecuted. Teachers are persecuted. I've never seen such hard-working people, such dedication in the face of such challenges. And for some reason, the public, and the media, just persecute them."

When she said that I thought back to a curriculum meeting I attended during the last year that I taught. The room was packed with teachers who came—voluntarily—to sit through a long, boring meeting after a full day of teaching.

Their feet hurt, their voices were tired, their backs ached, they were hungry and thirsty. They were not required to be there. They were not getting paid for it. They were there because they *cared* about that curriculum. They cared whether the children learned step A before they were taught step B. It *mattered* to them. Their families waited at home, supper not made, and still they sat through that three-hour meeting.

Those people are my heroes.

Teachers are feeling terribly beat-up right now. They are being forced by the government to teach in ways that go against their own best practices. Teachers with thirty years' experience and three degrees are being told they are not qualified.

They feel voiceless. They feel powerless.

Effective education reform will not happen until we see the issues clearly. But the public can't see them clearly because only one side of the story is being told. And so it is my mission to share with the public the real story of what it's like to teach school today.

Teachers must be empowered to speak their truths.

They must learn to trust their voices.

They must not be afraid to tell parents, administrators, legislators, and the media what is on their minds.

It's time for teachers to take back the profession.

DISCUSSION
QUESTIONS

Discussion Questions

Chapter 1

1. Who controls the public school system?
2. Who should control the public school system?
3. Are the best teacher qualities instinctual, or learned?
4. Is it appropriate to discipline a stranger's child?
5. Do you remember a teacher who had Super Powers?
6. Have you ever awed a child with your Super Powers?
7. Should teacher seniority be a factor in teaching assignments?
8. What kind of support do first year teachers need?
9. At what point in teacher education should the student teaching experience occur?
10. What can colleges do to better prepare teachers?
11. How can teachers show students they care without trying to be their best friends?
12. Should teachers "detach" from their students the way that doctors and surgeons do?
13. Should student teachers avoid the teachers' lounge?
14. Is the term "teachers' lounge" politically incorrect?
15. What more can be done to keep sexual predators out of schools?
16. What more can be done to protect innocent teachers from false accusations?
17. What qualities make for an effective in-service?

18. Describe the perfect in-service.
19. What are the symptoms of teacher burnout?
20. What can be done to rekindle the flame of a burned-out teacher?
21. Should the public school system have the power to force teacher retirement?
22. How do you recognize apathy in a teacher?
23. Describe the working conditions in a school.
24. How do those working conditions mesh with your personality?

Chapter 2

1. How do you make students like and respect you without giving in to their demands?
2. How much does the teacher influence learning?
3. Should students be "tracked" into classes according to ability?
4. Should Advanced Placement teaching positions be rotated among staff?
5. What can be done to improve the substitute teacher situation?
6. What kind of support does a substitute teacher need within the building?
7. How important are first impressions in the classroom?
8. What should be in a substitute teacher's emergency kit?
9. What's the solution to the tissue issue?
10. What is the school's responsibility in regards to health and hygiene?
11. What message do we send to kids when we allow PA interruptions?
12. How can we curb PA interruptions?
13. Should driver's training be part of the public school system?
14. Should the right to drive be tied to school attendance or academics?
15. How much does the group dynamic affect learning?
16. What can be done to improve the group dynamic of a class?
17. When did you discover that teachers are human?
18. What were the legends about some of your teachers?
19. What are the benefits of webcams in the classroom?
20. Are webcams in the classroom an invasion of privacy?
21. What is the weakest link in school security?
22. What are the most effective methods of school security?
23. Should teacher tenure be abolished?
24. What do you see as a fair teacher evaluation tool?

Chapter 3

1. Before break what is more appropriate, learning games or business as usual?
2. Should parties be allowed in the classroom?
3. How can we educate politicians about what schools really need?
4. How do we convince politicians to create education legislation that is not self-serving?
5. How can we limit the effect of politics on education?
6. What are the pros and cons of privatization?
7. Why are educators left out of the education reform conversation?
8. How can educators get into the education reform conversation?
9. What are the positive aspects of NCLB?
10. What needs to be changed in NCLB?
11. How much do official count days affect school cancellations?
12. Should teachers have to report when school is canceled?
13. What should be the rules about food in school?
14. Should the rules about food in school be set by teachers, or administrators?
15. Is the full moon phenomena fact, or fiction?
16. How contagious are student moods?
17. What are your hot weather strategies?
18. How do you handle student allergies?

Chapter 4

1. Should non-English-speaking students be mainstreamed?
2. How do you grade a non-English-speaking student?
3. What would you do with a student like Roberto?
4. Should students ever be allowed to sleep in class?
5. What measures can schools take to solve their bathroom issues?
6. Should state legislators be involved in school maintenance and discipline issues?
7. Should educators try to teach the value of "stuff"?
8. What's the solution to the "I don't have a pencil" claim?
9. Can organizational skills be taught, or are they inherent?

10. Should backpacks be banned for security or health reasons?
11. What are effective strategies for helping students through freshman year?
12. Should freshmen be housed away from upper and lower grades?
13. Could school districts eliminate busing at the high school level?
14. Should students have to pay to park in the student parking lot?
15. Describe a networking system among educators to help identify the shuffled children.
16. What can teachers do to help the shuffled children?
17. Why do so many teens think it is not "cool" to be smart?
18. How can we make academics "cool"?
19. What can we do to make sure the average child gets his due?
20. How can we help the average child find what makes her unique?
21. Should teachers and administrators cut seniors some slack?
22. What's the cure for senioritis?
23. On the last day of school, which is more appropriate, a party or a test?
24. How can we constructively channel seniors' energy on the last day of school?

Chapter 5

1. Do dress codes violate a student's freedom of expression?
2. How specific should dress codes be?
3. When it comes to dirty dancing, how dirty is too dirty?
4. What's the best way to handle dirty dancing at school dances?
5. What are the personality traits of a cutter?
6. To what extent should schools offer counseling or therapy?
7. Is homework obsolete?
8. Should the homework load be coordinated between teachers?
9. What are some strategies for teaching girls to support each other?
10. How has the women's movement affected girls today?
11. Why are there so few positive role models for girls?
12. Why are so many girls drawn to bad role models?
13. How can we teach girls the difference between popularity and achievement?
14. What new tradition could replace the homecoming queen tradition?

15. What can educators do to counter the music culture's attitude toward females?
16. How can educators get parents to help with student attitudes?
17. What are the pros and cons of same sex schools?
18. What are some cultural differences that affect education?
19. Should the public school system be a forum for any and all issues?
20. How does the issue of gender identity affect learning?
21. Should commercial vending machines be allowed in schools?
22. How responsible is the school system in the issue of childhood obesity?
23. Are virtual classes in support of, or in competition with, the public school system?
24. What is lacking in the virtual classroom experience?

Chapter 6

1. Is it possible to police impoliteness?
2. Is it the job of the public school system to try to improve society?
3. Is discipline ever cut and dried?
4. What kind of discipline support do teachers need?
5. Should administrators uphold discipline decisions under pressure of public opinion?
6. How do you convince a parent that discipline is a key to learning?
7. What is the cause of resistance in students?
8. What can be done to counter the resistance of students?
9. What does proper hallway behavior look like?
10. How would you go about taking back the halls?
11. When is suspension a viable option?
12. Are there any good alternatives to suspension?
13. Design an effective in-school suspension program.
14. Should parents be penalized when their child is suspended?
15. Can you make parents respect the drop-off /pick-up times of an elementary school?
16. Design the perfect tardy policy.
17. Design the perfect attendance policy.
18. Should student attendance affect grades?

19. How often, and to what extent, should teachers communicate with parents?
20. How do you tell parents that their child is lying?
21. Should sports be part of the school system, or a community or church activity?
22. Is it a right, or a privilege, to play on an athletic team?
23. What are the effects of a coach's leadership on an entire community?
24. What are the ramifications when a principal questions a teacher's judgment?

Chapter 7

1. Develop an effective script, or checklist, to use with parents at conferences.
2. Should students attend conferences with their parents?
3. Should teachers tell parents everything they know about their kids?
4. Is there such a thing as student–teacher confidentiality?
5. Can parents go too far in keeping tabs on their kids?
6. How accessible should schools be for parent visitation?
7. What is the perfect balance between parental neglect, and hovering?
8. How important is it for parents to teach self-sufficiency?
9. At what point should a principal step in between a teacher and a parent?
10. What are effective ways of dealing with harassing parents?
11. How has parental involvement improved the public school system?
12. How has parental involvement hurt the public school system?
13. How important to learning is quiet, contemplative time?
14. Describe other unmeasured impediments to learning.
15. Should districts ask students to participate in fundraisers?
16. Should education be funded privately, locally, federally, or by the state?
17. Is prom still a viable student activity?
18. Should prom be scaled down?
19. What are the alternatives to the small auditorium or the sports arena graduation?
20. Is there a way to control the crowd in a sports arena graduation?

Chapter 8

1. List several recent trends in education.
2. What are some effective relationship building strategies?
3. Are public schools their own worst enemy?
4. What factors contribute to a district's reputation?
5. How realistic is the idea of a lawyer in every school?
6. How can school districts function more proactively and less reactively?
7. How serious is the issue of grade inflation?
8. Are there situations where grade inflation can be justified?
9. Should students always be given the benefit of the doubt?
10. How much should a student's attitude about learning affect his grade?
11. Do more highly paid teachers deliver a better education?
12. Should the teacher pay scale depend on the subject being taught?
13. Are superintendent searches a worthwhile use of taxpayer money?
14. How much would you tell a superintendent interview team?
15. Is merit pay fair?
16. What should be the criteria for a merit pay system?
17. How do you feel about school districts that advertise?
18. What is the most important thing a parent should know about a school?
19. Should the school bus system be privatized?
20. Should parents have to pay to use the school bus system?
21. If your school building could talk, what would it say?
22. Who should pay to refurbish this country's public school buildings?
23. How have students changed over time?
24. Is the labeling of students prejudicial, or realistic?
25. To what extent should students be responsible for cleaning up after themselves?
26. Should students be required to clean the cafeteria?
27. Should a principal be a building leader, or an academic leader?
28. Can a principal with limited classroom experience fairly evaluate a teacher?
29. What are the biggest misconceptions about the teaching profession?
30. How has the public stereotyped teachers?
31. Is career education the responsibility of the public school system?
32. How can we better incorporate career education K–12?

Chapter 9

1. Can the No Child Left Behind Act save a Phase 5 school?
2. Describe the kind of help a Phase 5 school needs.
3. How can we get politicians to spend more time in public schools?
4. What would a politician be most surprised to learn about public schools?
5. Do you believe that all kids can learn?
6. Do you think that most educators believe that all kids can learn?
7. How can educators improve the culture of the nonlearner?
8. How should educators approach the mindset of the nonlearner?
9. What are the advantages and disadvantages of small classes?
10. How effective is the tutoring provision of NCLB?
11. How can educators hold the testing and tutoring industries accountable?
12. What are some assessment alternatives to the standardized test?
13. Are the needs of gifted and talented students being adequately met?
14. Should gifted and talented students receive as much funding as special education students?
15. How can educators enlighten the public about the big business connection?
16. How can educators "work" the big business connection?
17. What are some strategies for motivating students?
18. How can NCLB be improved to address the issue of nonmotivated students?
19. What are the qualities of a good teacher?
20. What are the qualities of a great teacher?
21. Is it logical for the public to hold teachers to higher standards than others?
22. What can be done to draw more extraordinary people to the teaching profession?
23. Design the perfect school.
24. How can we convince legislators to fund building repair?
25. How can educators show legislators what they need to be effective?
26. What would effective education reform look like?

Chapter 10

1. What would a nationwide grassroots education funding protest look like?
2. Is education a priority with most voters?
3. How can we mobilize the incredible organizational skills of educators?
4. Why are educators so often reluctant to speak up about their profession?
5. What creates the perfect teachable moment?
6. How can we cultivate a reverence for education?

About the Author

Her mother says she was a born teacher, and indeed Kelly Flynn did start teaching school at the age of five to a wide assortment of neighborhood kids. But she discovered a passion for news writing in Mrs. Webster's Beginning Journalism class her sophomore year, so after high school graduation she headed off to Michigan State University to major in journalism. She later decided to combine her two loves and changed her major to English Education with a minor in journalism.

She started teaching in 1981, advised student publications for fifteen years, earned the title of Certified Journalism Educator from the Journalism Education Association in 1990, and served as a publication judge for the National Scholastic Press Association from 1989 to 2002.

In 2002, Flynn left the classroom to pursue her love of journalism once again. For six years she has written a freelance weekly newspaper column for *The Flint Journal*, covering education from an insider's point of view. The column also ran in the *Jackson Citizen Patriot* for three years.